Library of
Davidson College

Ralph Crane and Some Shakespeare First Folio Comedies

RALPH CRANE
AND
SOME SHAKESPEARE
FIRST FOLIO COMEDIES

T. H. HOWARD-HILL

Published for the Bibliographical Society of
the University of Virginia

The University Press of Virginia
Charlottesville

THE UNIVERSITY PRESS OF VIRGINIA
Copyright © 1972 by the Rector and Visitors
of the University of Virginia

First published 1972

ISBN: 0-8139-0410-2
Library of Congress Catalog Card Number: 72-82769
Printed in the United States of America

To

Alice Walker

CONTENTS

Preface	ix
List of tables in the text	xiii
Cue titles and abbreviations	xv
1. INTRODUCTION	1
2. CRANE'S DRAMATIC TRANSCRIPTS	9
3. CRANE'S SCRIBAL PRACTICES IN HIS DRAMATIC TRANSCRIPTS	16
4. CRANE'S INFLUENCE IN THE FIVE COMEDIES	69
5. THE FIVE COMEDIES: CONCLUSION	104
NOTES	141
APPENDICES	160
Bibliography	173
Index	181

PREFACE

In the last half-century, many learned critics detected signs of Crane's influence in five of the Folio comedies and the present study of this aspect of The Tempest, Two Gentlemen of Verona, Merry Wives of Windsor, Measure for Measure, and Winter's Tale (the only texts implied by the somewhat general title of this book) does not materially alter the common opinion. I did not expect that it would. What I have set out to do here is to describe Crane's habits as precisely as the extant dramatic transcripts allow and to bring the relevant information to bear on the texts and problems with which he has been associated. The five comedies have not hitherto been considered together in relation to their probable common origin from transcripts in Crane's hand. By examining the five comedies together in light of his habits and the extent to which they varied over the years, I have endeavoured to supply editors with two kinds of information. In the following pages I show that he prepared copy for Tmp., TGV, Wiv., MM and WT: I believe that this can be stated as fact and that, therefore, editors must take account of his habits when they study the texts of these plays. I have shown that his habits changed during the period

covered by his extant transcripts and that although he
constantly favoured, for instance, relatively heavy
punctuation, variation of his practices makes it
necessary to allow for the period in his development as
a copyist of literary manuscripts when a particular
transcript may have been made.

Some attempt has been made to identify the
characteristics of the five comedies which owe more
to transcription by Crane than to the author, or to
setting into type by Jaggard's compositors. A fairly
detailed examination of the compositors of the Folio
comedies assisted the later part of this investigation,
but because it was not of main importance here and has
a somewhat wider interest in another Shakespearian
context, it is to appear separately in Studies in
Bibliography, 1973. I have not been able to do more
than touch on substantive matters of text which are of
primary importance for editors, but I have supplied them
with a notion of how the five comedies differ as a
group from the other Folio comedies, and how much or how
little of their shared characteristics may be attributed
to the compositors, and I have also given a view of the
special orthographical characteristics of the five
comedies which will serve to assist correction of the
text.

This work was carried out during the last stages
of the editing of the Oxford Shakespeare Concordances.
These, although they were intended to supply quickly
simple working tools for detailed textual and linguistic

PREFACE　　　　　　　　xi

investigations, came to occupy most of my time. The
results of the present investigation were accepted as
fulfillment of the thesis requirement for the Oxford
D. Phil., but I do not regard work on the larger
question of Crane's influence as completed. Further
time and patient study is required, however, to apply
the materials which have become available to me
(principally through my association with the Oxford
University Computing Laboratory) to analysis of the
substantives of these texts and to study whether Crane
had a greater part in the preparation of Folio copy.
2 Henry IV is a text which demands closer examination
for possible Crane influence. This study depends so
greatly on correct identification of compositorial
stints in the Folio and of the habits of the individual
compositors, matters which are laborious and time-
consuming to determine, that I have taken little notice
of the Folio histories and tragedies here. The final
account of Crane's influence on Folio texts should be
based on examination of the whole First Folio.

　　I first began to work on Crane under the supervision of Dr. S. G. Culliford, of Victoria University
of Wellington, whose advice I recall with respect and
gratitude. My obligation to my supervisor and friend,
Dr. Alice Walker, formerly Reader in Textual Criticism
in Oxford University, is so great that it can be truly
appreciated only by those who have benefited as I have
from her supervision and advice. With her help I
obtained the support of the Clarendon Press to prepare

Shakespearian texts for computation. Two substantial grants towards this work from the British Academy are also acknowledged with appreciation. Not all the fruits of their beneficence are embodied in the present work. A summer spent as Research Fellow at the Shakespeare Institute, University of Birmingham, in 1964, and a N.I.R.N.S. Fellowship from the Atlas Computing Laboratory, Chilton, supplied essential support at the beginning of the investigation, and this was maintained by the Director and Staff of the Computing Laboratory, Oxford, who provided facilities for data preparation and computation from 1965. No thorough study of Crane and the five comedies could have been made without the friendly offices of many individuals and institutions, whose help I am pleased to acknowledge here, but my chief obligation is to the secretarial staff and Delegates of the Clarendon Press, Oxford, for their continuing aid and advice. I am also grateful to Professor Fredson Bowers for his kind offer to suggest the manuscript for publication by the University of Virginia Bibliographical Society, and to the Society for publishing it. Finally, the manuscript has been greatly improved by the meticulous scrutiny of D. G. Neill to whom I am much indebted for his comments and corrections.

Swansea   T. H. H.

LIST OF TABLES

Marks of punctuation in Crane transcripts — 32

Variants of potential influence on the metre in *Game*, acts 1-3 — 47-51

Marks of punctuation in ten Folio comedies — 82

Crane spellings in the comedies — 100-1

Other possibly significant spellings in the comedies — 101-2

Spellings ending in -nes and -nesse in the five comedies — 102

Tempest: readings accepted by the New Arden editor — 110-11

Two Gentlemen: readings accepted by the New Arden editor — 115-16

Merry Wives: readings accepted by the New Arden editor — 120-1

Measure for Measure: readings accepted by the New Arden editor — 124-6

Winter's Tale: readings accepted by the New Arden editor — 131-2

APPENDICES

1. Variant readings in *Game* Lansdowne and Malone — 160-1
2. Conjectural emendations in *The Witch* — 161-3
3. Variants in *Demetrius* and *The Humourous Lieutenant* — 163-5
4. Variants of compositor B's spellings in *Twelfth Night* — 165-6
5. Variants of compositor B's spellings in *Err.* — 166-7
6. Variants of compositor B's spellings in *Shr.* — 167-9
7. Variants of compositor B's spellings in *Tmp.*, *Wiv.*, *MM* and *WT* — 169-72

CUE TITLES AND ABBREVIATIONS

Barnavelt   Sir John van Olden Barnavelt, by
(Bar.)   Fletcher and Massinger. A Crane
                   transcript, 1619. (B.M. MS. Add.
                   18653).

Demetrius   Demetrius and Enanthe [or, The
(Dem.)   Humourous Lieutenant] by Fletcher.
                   A Crane transcript, 1625.
                   (Brogyntyn MS. 42).

Game   A Game at Chess, by Middleton.

Game Trinity   Trinity College, Cambridge, MS. in
(GmT)   Middleton's holograph. (Trinity
                   College, Cambridge, MS. O.2.66)

Game Bridgewater Huntington Library MS. transcribed
(GmB)   by Middleton and two scribes.
                   (Henry E. Huntington Library,
                   San Marino, Calif. MS.).

Game Folger   Folger Shakespeare Library MS.,
(GmF)   transcribed by Crane, 1624.
                   (Folger MS. 7043).

Game Lansdowne   British Museum MS., transcribed by
(GmL)   Crane, 1624. (B.M. MS. Lansdowne
                   690).

Game Malone   Bodleian Library MS., a Crane
(GmM)   transcript, 1624/5. (Bodleian
                   Library MS. Malone 25).

Pleasure   Pleasure Reconciled to Virtue, by
(PRV)   Jonson. A Crane transcript, 1618.
                   (Chatsworth MS.).

Song in several parts   Middleton's 'invention',
(SSP)   transcribed by Crane, 1622. (P.R.O.
                   MS. State papers, domestic, v. 129,
                   doc. 53).

Witch   The Witch, by Middleton. A Crane
(Wit.)   A Crane transcript, 1624. (Bodleian
                   Library MS. Malone 12).

CUE TITLES AND ABBREVIATIONS

The abbreviations of the titles of Shakespeare's plays are those which have recently been adopted by the Shakespeare Association of America, <u>Shakespeare Quarterly</u>, and the New Variorum Committee. References to the First Folio use Folio through-line-numbers as provided by the Norton facsimile of the First Folio, and the Oxford Shakespeare concordances. Act and scene references have been taken from the edition referred to in the discussion.

Ralph Crane and Some Shakespeare First Folio Comedies

1. INTRODUCTION

My aim here is to examine, as thoroughly as the available evidence allows, the opinion now generally held that Ralph Crane prepared Jaggard's copy for five of the First Folio comedies: <u>The Tempest</u>, <u>The Two Gentlemen of Verona</u>, <u>The Merry Wives of Windsor</u>, <u>Measure for Measure</u>, and <u>The Winter's Tale</u>.

Crane, a professional scrivener first identified by F. P. Wilson in 1926,[1] seems to have had a close association with the King's Men on the evidence of his own words in the Preface to his <u>Works of Mercy</u>. This is substantiated by the number of dramatic transcripts now recognised as in his hand, but although it is comparatively simple to identify a handwriting, it is more complex to get a clear idea of a printer's copy set up by compositors who might or might not have reproduced its characteristics.[2]

The interest of Ralph Crane for students of early seventeenth century drama is most readily conveyed by these lines from the Preface to his <u>Works of Mercy</u>:

>   And some imployment hath my vsefull <u>Pen</u>
>   Had 'mongst those ciuill, well-deseruing <u>men</u>,
>   That grace the <u>Stage</u> with honour and <u>delight</u>,
>   Of whose true honesties I much could write,
>   But will comprise't (as in a Caske of Gold)
>   Vnder the <u>Kingly Seruice</u> they doe hold.[3]

This passage, made familiar by Wilson and Greg, is the only explicit testimony of Crane's association with the King's Men. All else must be drawn from the obscure outlines of his biography and inferred from the eight surviving dramatic manuscripts in his handwriting. He has two claims to serious attention. The first is the chance that he was the book-keeper to the King's Men, or, if not that, closely associated with the Company in another way. The other is his supposed connection with the five Folio comedies, and the possibility that his influence on the Folio was greater than is commonly thought. These matters of interest are connected for, if he was the Company's book-keeper, he would have had opportunity to be involved in the editing of the Folio. On the other hand, if his relations with the Players were not close, it would not be surprising to find little trace of his hand in the Folio. It is worthwhile, therefore, to look attentively at any evidence which might link him with the King's Men, before beginning the examination of the Folio comedies supposed to have been printed from his transcripts.

His own claim in <u>The Works of Mercy</u> of 'some imployment ... 'mongst' the players falls far short of a statement that he was ever a member or employee of the Company, as the book-keeper must certainly have been, and shows only that he did 'some' work for the players. The transcripts later than <u>Barnavelt</u> which have dedications suggest that most of his work was undertaken for individual playwrights rather than for the Company, though, to be sure, these need not be exclusive and his relationship with the King's Men may have changed between

1619 and 1625. Some confusion about this arose from Wilson's early article on Crane: even in 'Shakespeare and the "New Bibliography"' his final opinion is not altogether clearly expressed. However, recent opinion has been satisfied to accept, with Greg, that Crane's association with the Company was not formal: he was not, on the face of it, the book-keeper.[4] His personal relations with writers for the Company, such as Middleton, must have been close, however, as witness his three transcripts of <u>Game</u> made while the players were in trouble with the Privy Council, the prompt-book with the King, and the author in hiding against a warrant of arrest.[5]

It would not be necessary to discuss the question further were it not for Crane's transcript of Fletcher and Massinger's <u>Sir John van Olden Barnavelt</u>. This must have been made for use as a prompt-book between July 14th, 1619, and August 14th, when it was prohibited by the Bishop of London.[6] It contains the notes of actors' names and stage properties usually accepted as evidence of adaptation for use as a prompt-book. What is important here is whether the added and unmistakably prompt stage-directions are in Crane's handwriting. Greg thought that they were. If Greg's view is correct, Crane must have been the book-keeper, and it would be possible to argue that he had a closer relationship and a more important function with the Company than many scholars allow. As Greg does not examine <u>Barnavelt</u> in detail elsewhere, it is useful to quote his words:

> ... many additional directions, including a
> number of actors' names, have been supplied
> in a much rougher hand. In the ensuing
> notes this hand has been treated, for the
> sake of distinction, as different from the
> scribe's: but in many instances the hand is
> in fact certainly the same, and probably it
> is so in all.[7]

Greg did not say which stage-directions led him to this conclusion. However, his identification of the hands may be questioned, as inspection of his own transcript of a page of Barnavelt, his plate 5, shows. The direction 'A Bar brought in' which he prints as in the hand of the book-keeper is in Crane's handwriting, that is, the writing of the body of the text.[8] These words need only be compared with 'Barre' and 'Daunce' above for the difference of the hands to be patent, and further confirmation is provided by comparison of the two 'Daunce's on the page. Indeed all the notes of actors' names and properties, save a few which shall be discussed below, are in a hand which has few points of similarity with Crane's and which is not found in any of his other dramatic transcripts.

There are, to be sure, some directions in Crane's handwriting which may be those Greg had in mind. For instance, on f. 21, there is the direction, 'Enter wife, aboue', and other locations are mentioned in stage-directions in his hand on f. 4^V ('at dore'), f. 9^V ('on $\overset{e}{y}$ walls'), f. 19 ('in his Studdy'), and elsewhere. In other directions properties are noted, e.g., on f. 21 ('wth Bowghs & flowres'), f. 24 ('wth Peares') and f. 27^V ('A Scaffold put out') but such directions are not unusual in author's papers, whence Crane may have copied

them. Other directions show that he sometimes took his
cue from the dialogue, if he and not the author was
responsible for these directions. On f. 21^v where the
text reads 'now for the <u>Daunce</u>, Boyes', Crane has written
'<u>Daunce</u>' as a direction in the right-hand margin. The
book-keeper was not satisfied with this and replaced it
with the same direction a few lines lower. Similarly, on
f. 25, 1.2584, which reads 'bring Chaires there for their
Lordships', is accompanied by the direction '2. <u>Chaires</u>'
in the right margin. An entrance a few lines before
shows that only two chairs would be needed. Another
example occurs on f. 20 where beside the line 'give me
some wyne' the scribe has written '<u>Enter Seru^t. wth
wine</u>'; the book-keeper crossed out the last two words
and wrote '<u>Ent: wth wyn</u>' three lines below. The
directions in Crane's handwriting which go beyond what
can reasonably be attributed to his copy have been drawn
from the text, and these directions, almost without
exception, the revising book-keeper replaced by other
directions of similar intent.[9]

More recently Greg cited <u>Barnavelt</u> to illustrate
the book-keeper's concern with necessary stage properties.
A direction on f. 27 reads '<u>Enter Prouost | Sold^s. &
Execu^{rs} | wth a Coffin | & a Gibbett.</u>' Miss Frijlinck
noted her impression that the last two lines were 'added
in a different hand' (p. 78) but Greg noted the addition
only of '<u>& a Gibbett</u>': later, however, he returned to
Miss Frijlinck's view.[10] No-one would contradict Greg
on such a matter lightly, but long familiarity with Crane's
handwriting leads me to disagree. The stage-direction
is in Crane's hand throughout. The slope and size of the

letters, however, suggest that the last three words were added after the first part of the direction had been written. This may have been when Crane saw later from his copy that a scaffold was required.

The most that need be said here of the directions in Barnavelt is that Crane perhaps anticipated the directions that the book-keeper would eventually supply. He did not take this very far and the revision, together with the addition of names of actors, shows that his directions were little help to the unidentified King's Men's book-keeper of the time. Barnavelt, then, offers no evidence to suggest that Crane did more than make the prompt-book for the book-keeper to mark up for performance. If his influence is to be found in the Folio, it is fairly certain that he was undertaking to prepare Jaggard's copy for the real 'editor', if there was one, of the Folio.[11]

His influence on the five comedies has often been referred to since Dover Wilson's first discussion of it in 1931, following a reference to the possibility in F. P. Wilson's article of 1926. Sir Walter Greg had earlier identified the hands of Barnavelt and Middleton's Witch as Crane's and most of what is known about Crane's life and works had been drawn together by F. P. Wilson in 1926. Dover Wilson thought that the numerous parentheses common to Crane's transcripts and certain Folio comedies made it likely that this scribe had prepared the printer's copy. A long drawn out discussion of the significance of the 'massed' entries in some early texts, including Crane's Malone transcript of Game, in which

Greg, F. P. Wilson, R. C. Bald, R. C. Rhodes and Dover Wilson were the protagonists, finally determined that such directions did not indicate that the texts had been 'assembled' from players' parts but were simply a characteristic of Crane's manuscription.[12] Greg later discussed the relevance of the 'Jonsonian' elision which often occurs in Crane transcripts, particularly in the later transcripts which were made for presentation to patrons, and his 1955 conclusion about Crane's responsibility in the editing of the Folio is not likely to be materially altered.[13]

So far as Crane's influence on particular texts goes, however, the matter is not settled. Wilson cautioned that 'as this scribe's habits have not been yet examined with any care or properly compared with those of other scribes of about the same date, speculation is still hazardous'.[14] Recently, however, some editors of volumes of the New Arden Shakespeare have supplied their readers with more detailed discussions of his scribal peculiarities, sometimes after independent examination of his transcripts, and have given some account of what may be characteristic of these in some Folio texts. These surveys are all the more valuable because the editors have been able to make allowance for the varying habits of the Folio compositors who, perhaps, set Crane's transcripts into type. Nevertheless, within the limited space and time at their disposal, the New Arden editors could not examine all aspects of these matters in adequate detail. Crane's transcripts are so extensive and the complexity of relating his scribal habits to the practices of the Folio compositors is so great that there is still much to be said on the question of his influence in the Folio. There are, too, Folio texts other than the five comedies in which some editors have detected his influence, and, doubtless, if this is to be found in the Folio at all, his presence might subsequently be noticed in places hitherto unremarked.[15] But at the moment, the inadequacy of knowledge of his habits is sufficient reason to restrict the present examination to the comedies of the Folio.

2. CRANE'S DRAMATIC TRANSCRIPTS

Readers have become more familiar with the later Crane transcripts from their Malone Society editions than the early transcripts which have not been recently edited. These are so markedly calligraphic in character that it is easy to conclude that all his transcripts are elaborately set out and show the parentheses, apostrophes and such scribal characteristics as the 'double hyphen' noted by the Malone Society editors. Such is not the case. No single manuscript shows all the characteristics which are now called Crane's, and the care with which he set out the text varied according to the purpose for which or reader for whom he made the copy. Since the most important question is the kind of manuscript which might have been sent to Jaggard, it is helpful to look more closely at all Crane's dramatic transcripts to see whether one or any number of them might serve as model for further study of the Folio comedies.[16]

Jonson's Pleasure Reconciled to Virtue of 1618 is the earliest Crane transcript that is known. It is a careful and elegantly-written copy, presumably made under Jonson's supervision, showing few of the scribal exuberances that appear in Witch, Demetrius, and the later Game transcripts. It is probably mere accident that his earliest surviving transcript is this Jonsonian composition. Nevertheless, whether or not Jonson initiated Crane into the art of literary transcription, there are conspicuous similarities between the general features of their manuscripts. Instances are the 'Jonsonian' apostrophes and the 'massed entries' adapted from a classical convention.[17] Jonson's holograph of The Masque of Queens (1609) has double hyphens throughout, it shows the diæresis in such words as 'Poëms', the circumflex over 'ô', the digraph in Latin-derived spellings like 'præscribe' and Ægipts', and the apostrophe after vowels in possessive singulars like 'Pluto's'. All these have their counterpart in Crane's transcripts.[18] Jonson favoured the marking of sententia by introductory quotation marks, a practice common in printed works of the period; there is an instance of this in Crane's Folger transcript of Game, and many in the first quarto of The Duchess of Malfi which was printed from a Crane transcript.[19] It is not difficult to imagine that Jonson's Folio of 1616, in which the plays were preceded by 'Names of the Actors' and locality indications and regularly divided into acts and scenes, must have supplied useful example to a scribe who sought a model for his literary transcripts. The similarity of their scribal habits should not be urged too strongly: Crane need not have been influenced by Jonson for spellings like 'pretious' and 'antient' which are sometimes found in his transcripts, or for digraphs in words like 'præscribe', when he transcribed manuscripts for Middleton, for Middleton too favoured such spellings.

Jonson's masque, like all Crane's transcripts before 1625, has no dedication. It was apparently transcribed for or just after the performance on January 6th, 1618, although whether for one of the performers or as a presentation copy, or both, there is no evidence to show. In this it is similar to the transcript of Middleton's 'invention' for presentation before the Lord Mayor of London, A Song in Several Parts, which is a less elaborate transcript. It was probably written for performance at Easter, 1622. Crane's prompt-book of Barnavelt in 1619, as has already been seen, is another transcript for which his services must have been engaged. Not until the Game of Chess transcripts of 1624-5 do Crane's manuscripts begin to show clear signs of preparation for closet reading. From evidence of the watermarks, the transcript of The Witch is dated around this time:[20] it must at least have been made before Middleton's death on July 4th, 1627, or Crane would not have copied out the author's dedication to Thomas Holmes. The Folger transcript of Game was copied while the play was still running for it is dated August 13th, 1624. In appearance it is more workmanlike than calligraphic and resembles Barnavelt rather than, say, Demetrius, but with Witch, it is the only transcript with running-titles. Whatever the significance of this fact (and in Witch, a presentation copy, the running-titles must have been for embellishment rather than a guide for the printer), Folger Game was a manuscript over whose accuracy the author took some care. This can be seen from Middleton's manuscript corrections in the first part of the transcript. The other Game transcripts are of different character. Game Lansdowne, which was dated simply '1624', presents a good text,

attractively set out; there is no dedication. Game
Malone, the text of which is closely related to that of
the Lansdowne manuscript and seems to have been prepared
after it, gives a much abbreviated text in which the
stage-directions have been massed after a literary convention. It contains a dedication in Middleton's hand
referring to it as a New Year gift, from which the manuscript may be dated 1625. Crane's last known dramatic
transcript is Fletcher's Demetrius and Enanthe which has
the first of Crane's own dedications: Fletcher had died
in August, 1625, and the dedication is dated November
27th, 1625. Thenceforth, Crane's transcripts of poetry
collections were to bear dedications which he had
composed himself.

These notes are brief because the manuscripts to
which they refer have already been described at fair
length by their recent editors, and my fresh examination
of some of their peculiarities is reserved to a later
chapter. What must be understood at once, however, is
the extent to which a transcript like Barnavelt differs
from Demetrius, the transcript which shows Crane at his
most accomplished. Differences arise not only because
Crane became more experienced and therefore surer in his
handling of the text, but also, because the later manuscripts were written under different circumstances and
for a different purpose. A prompt-book such as Barnavelt
would need to supply a correct text, but no exceptional
care need be taken over metre and elisions which were to
show how a line was to be read, for only the book-keeper
would read the prompt-book, and the players would speak
their lines as their art or the book-keeper instructed

them. The stage-directions would need to make clear who came on, and when, and sometimes, whence the actors were to make their entrances, but they need not be full. So long as the characters, entrances and stage properties were correctly indicated, the stage-directions need offer little aid to the inner eye of imagination. Calligraphic curlicues, non-functional italicisation and distinctive and ornate handwriting would have been unnecessary. On the other hand, a manuscript prepared for a reader would be enhanced by careful distinction of acts and scenes, elaboration of calligraphic features like ornamental initials and capitals, lavish use of italics in the dialogue, and the provision of catchwords to lead the eye, and the silent reader would be further assisted by the scribe's careful attention to elision and metre. If the scribe were to use the stage-directions to supply what the reader missed from performance, this would seem a helpful and desirable aspect of his task.

It is difficult to resist the conclusion that as Crane became accustomed to transcribing literary manuscripts so he became more dependent on calligraphic means to commend his transcripts and himself to the attention of patrons and clients whose bounty he sought in his old age. Fidelity to his original copy was not one of his foremost concerns. There is no evidence, for instance, that he ever checked his transcripts against their original, or did more than correct the slips of his pen when he was aware of them. So far as can be seen the improvements were orthographical rather than textual in a stricter sense, though the cumulative effect of such attentions cannot be lightly dismissed. The *Game* transcripts supply the clearest illustrations of his sophisticating influence on the text: the discussion in the next chapter contains many specific instances of his interference with his copy.

If Crane did prepare copy for the Folio, it must, with the exception of WT, have been before February, 1622, when Hinman dates the start of work on the printing.[21] The most calligraphic transcripts are later than this. Nevertheless, any transcript he made for the Folio was, he knew, to be read rather than used in the theatre: it was not likely to have escaped the attentions which he gave the later Game transcripts. Further, if he was copying from his own transcript, his influence on the metre and orthography would be so much the greater as he would not have been constrained by the author's practices. The text itself, one might hazard, would show the usual corruption from copy to copy. Therefore, the extant transcripts which offer the best illustration of what his copy for the Folio may have been like are possibly not those prepared for performance, like Barnavelt and Pleasure, or written under supervision like Game Folger, but the more calligraphic transcripts, Game Lansdowne and Malone, Witch and Demetrius, presentation copies intended for private reading. It is certain, however, as subsequent discussion shall demonstrate, that there is no extant transcript which is like Crane's possible Folio copy in all its features, and that Folio copy is quite likely to have been less calligraphic in character than his later transcripts, if only because it was prepared before he had had much experience of literary transcription.

Moreover, it is not known whether anyone connected with the King's Men read the transcripts he may have made for the Folio, or what instructions he may have been given. <u>Game</u> Folger does suggest that many matters with which modern textual scholarship is concerned would not have received much attention, if attention was paid to them at all. Sir Walter Greg suggested that <u>Tmp</u>. was prepared by Crane as a model for the Folio. If that is probable, then it is doubtful whether the text benefited from the scribe's expertise.^{22}

The features of Crane transcripts of most importance to editors of Shakespeare are those which could have been reproduced in type; evidence of Crane's characteristic ? or double hyphen should not be expected in the Folio for these are calligraphic peculiarities which the compositors would not attempt to reproduce. Irrelevant too are such purely calligraphic features of his transcripts as ornamental flourishes and ruling. On the other hand it is useful to consider in some detail how he presented act and scene divisions, stage-directions, speech-prefixes, italicisation and capitalisation as well as his spellings, elisions, compounds, contractions, treatment of metre and of prose and verse. Most important of all to know is whether substantive errors in texts which were printed from his transcripts must be laid to his charge or the Folio compositors! Therefore an impression of his fidelity to copy and of the kinds of error to which he was prone must be gained from the texts of which alternative or edited versions exist.

3. CRANE'S SCRIBAL PRACTICES IN HIS DRAMATIC TRANSCRIPTS

Crane's handwriting interests the student of penmanship for its own sake: he wrote a good secretary hand and a particularly fine Italian hand which he used, for instance, for differentiating songs and letters from the dialogue. The editors of the Malone Society editions of Witch and Demetrius have observed how difficult it is to distinguish the different styles and mixtures of English and Italian script in those transcripts, particularly as Crane's secretary hand often contains individual letters which are more italic in style than English. His hand is, in fact, 'mixed' rather than pure secretary. It is especially difficult to decide whether he intended words beginning with L, M, N, W, and Y to be regarded as capitalised or not, and very often the relative size of the letter or the relation of the word to the context rather than distinctive majuscule form determines an editor's judgement. This bears on the present investigation in two ways. Firstly, generalisations about Crane's characteristic use of capitals and italics, or his habits in word-division or elision, depend on how the transcripts have been interpreted, and on how consistently the graphical forms have been treated from text to text. Secondly, a compositor who had a Crane transcript in front of him as copy would have had similar difficulty in deciding whether his copy intended a capital letter

or the like. A compositor would have applied a rather
different set of orthographical conventions to his copy
and any obscurities in Crane's manuscript would not have
affected him in exactly the same way as they do a modern
editor. Nor is it likely, as Moxon shows, that a
compositor would have spent much time in puzzling over
the accidentals of his copy. Nevertheless, he would have
accepted some guidance from his copy in matters of
orthography, if only to avoid having to make frequent
decisions on points of typographical styling. The substantive readings of Crane transcripts are generally not
in doubt but sometimes it is not easy to decide what he
intended for the accidentals. Although accidentals
become less important for an editor once the Folio texts
printed from Crane transcripts have been identified, they
do assist identification of his influence, and it is
therefore useful to gain a clear notion of the general
characteristics of his transcripts.[23]

His transcripts were usually written in the English
secretary hand, with the Italian hand used for headings
and proper nouns or other words in the text which he
wished to emphasise. He also varied his italic with a
heavier pressure on his pen or by writing words larger
than the surrounding text to produce what may be called
a 'bold italic', possibly with a different pen. This
served to emphasise particular words in passages of italic
like letters or stage-directions just as the italic hand
was used to emphasise words in the dialogue written in his
secretary hand. An illustration of this can be seen in
the act and scene heading and stage-direction on p. 1 of
<u>Demetrius</u> in the facsimile reproduced in the Malone

Society edition. There 'Actus' and 'Sce^a.' are written in a heavier hand than the lighter, more cursive italic 'Primus' and 'pri^a.' which follow. The similar heading in <u>Witch</u> shows the same variation. This also appears in the list of characters which precedes <u>Witch</u> to emphasise 'Rauenna' and the other names.^{24} Of greater interest are such stage-directions as that on p. 78 of <u>Game</u> Lansdowne where the stage-direction which describes the dumb show may be transcribed thus:

<u>Sce^a. 3^a. Enter ye Black Q^s. Pawne (wth a Tapo^r in her hand) and Conducts the White Q^s. Pawne (in her Night Attire) into one Chamber:</u> ...^{25}

There is also a corresponding use of an English script which might, in some circumstances, be mistaken for the emphasised italic. The italic dedication to <u>Witch</u> shows 'Thomas Holmes' in this hand.^{26} Most of the letter forms are Italian in character but perpendicularity and other distinct letter forms show that the scribe intended a variation. I shall refer to this as 'bold English' although a more suitable term might be 'perpendicular italic'. In this example the 'English' characteristics are not strongly marked. Better examples can be found in Crane's dedications to British Museum MS. Harleian 3357 and Add. 34752, and Bodleian MS. Rawlinson D 301, where this script is used for contrast with the bold italic he also affected for display. The hand can also be found in stage-directions: <u>Game</u> Lansdowne presents an example on p. 63 where in the direction '— Musick | <u>ye Black B^{ps} Pawne | Enters</u> ...' the first word is manifestly not intended to be read as italic.

SCRIBAL PRACTICES IN TRANSCRIPTS   19

The purport of this is that Crane used a variety of hands and styles of writing to distinguish different words of the text. If a compositor paid any attention to such distinctions, it would have been difficult for him to decide whether a distinction was intended in a particular instance, and, having noticed a variation of hand, he would have had to decide whether and, if so, how to represent it in type. In this he would have been guided by typographical considerations.

ACT AND SCENE HEADINGS

Acts and scenes are correctly marked in all Crane's transcripts of plays, usually with a formula like 'Actus Quartus | Sce.^{a} 2^a. Enter ...'. Minor variations of spelling do not appear to be significant. Game Folger and Witch also have 'Finis Actus Secundij' or the like at the end of each act; this was Middleton's practice in Game Trinity, but Crane did not follow him in using 'Incipit Actus ...' for the act headings. There is an interesting stage-direction at 2.2.108 in the Folger transcript where the scribe has inserted a new scene heading for Middleton's 'Enter wh. qs. pawne'. Because both the White and the Black houses were on stage at that point he lists them: 'Enter (seu[er]ally) wh. King: Q: B^p. | Duke: Knight: Pawnes: & Q.^{s} Pawne: and Bl. | King. Q. B^p. &c.'. This stage-direction has the effect of masking the separate entrance of the White Queen's Pawn. There is no similar direction in any other text of Game.

Apart from these minor points, only in Game Malone, where Crane does not start the main entrances with

'Enter', is there anything remarkable about the principal stage-directions with act and scene headings. Here the names of the characters who are to appear in a scene are listed together at the beginning, and entrances for the characters who come on later are usually not separately noted at the appropriate point. The stage-direction which heads the Induction is not massed: there is a marginal entry for the White and Black houses at 1. 53. The Malone transcript also has an exit for the Black Bishop's Pawne at 1. 109 and 'Enter agen' at 1. 114 of 4.1, but whether Crane intended to preserve directions which he thought were essential for the action of the stage or whether he copied them from his source inadvertently cannot be shown.

These listing or massed entries were used earlier by some English writers of comedies like Lyly, probably under the influence of continental editions of the old Greek and Latin comedians which supplied only a list of the speakers at the head of scenes (which were not numbered) and did not mark internal entrances or exits. This system was adopted by Jonson, first in the quartos of Cynthia's Revels and Poetaster where acts and scenes were numbered and a number of internal entries and exits were given, and later with greater regularity in the quartos of Sejanus, Volpone, The Alchemist and in the 1616 Folio in which many more scenes are marked.[27] Dover Wilson and R. C. Rhodes favoured the view that these massed entries in Folio texts implied that they had been put together from the playhouse plot and actors' parts, but although their case was supported with arguments from other features of such Shakespearian texts as MV, the theory of assembled texts has long since fallen into disrepute. In <u>Game</u> Malone the massed entries were superimposed on the normal English arrangement of acts and scenes and although Jonson's Folio seems to have been influential, Crane apparently did not properly understand the correct use of the convention. All the post-Jonsonian texts with massed stage-directions have been associated with Crane and this must be taken as a characteristic of his. Apart from <u>TGV</u>, <u>Wiv</u>. and <u>WT</u>, massed entries are found in <u>Game</u> Malone and the first quarto of <u>The Duchess of Malfi</u> which was printed from his transcript.[28]

STAGE DIRECTIONS

During the course of the controversy which arose from Dover Wilson's theory of assembling, R. C. Bald noted that some of the directions in <u>Game</u> Malone were so descriptive in character as to make it hardly likely that they would have been preserved in actors' parts, or the plot.[29] Verbal differences amongst the stage-directions in the <u>Game</u> manuscripts suggest too that they owe something to transcription. Directions taken from <u>Game</u> Lansdowne and Malone are especially instructive here since they were almost certainly prepared from the same manuscript.

LANSDOWNE	MALONE	
Ind. 54 <u>Enter $\overset{e}{y}$ white House | & $\overset{e}{y}$ Black, (as in Order | of the Game)</u>	<u>Enter (seuerally) $\overset{e}{y}$ | white-house, & Black | (in order of the</u>	<u>House | Game</u>

This direction does not occur in <u>Game</u> Trinity or the

Bridgewater transcript, or in the two 1625 quartos which Bald associates with them. Crane seems to have been responsible for 'seuerally' at least; it is found also in his Folger transcript and in Q3 which is thought to have been printed from another of his transcripts.[30]

LANSDOWNE	MALONE
3.3 Musick | $\overset{e}{y}$ Black B^{ps}. Pawne | Enters, (as in an Appa-|rition) richelie habited.	Musique: | The Bl. B^{ps}. Pawne (as | in an Apparition) Comes | richely habited.
4.3 ...Pawne (wth a Tapo^r in her | hand) and Conducts the White Q^s. Pawne (in her | Night Attire) into one Chamber: And then Conuaies the | Black B^s. Pawne (in his Night habit) into an other | Chamber: So putts out...	...Pawne (with a Taper) Conducts | $\overset{e}{y}$ Wh. Queenes-Pawne (in her night attire) into one | Chamber; Then Conuaies $\overset{e}{y}$ Bl. B^{ps}. Pawne, into | an other Chamber, So puts out. ...[31]
5.1.40 Musick | an Altar discouered wth | Tapers on it: and diuers Images about it.	An Altar | discovered with | Tapors on it: and | Images about it.
5.3.198 The Bagg opens, | & $\overset{e}{y}$ Black lost | Pawnes appeere in it	The Bagg | opens, & the | Black-Side | put into it

The variations here amount to little more than some rearrangement of words and substitution of epithets, with the loss of a few connectives, but this is enough, with the omission of 'in his Night habit' in the third

SCRIBAL PRACTICES IN TRANSCRIPTS 23

direction and the significance for staging of the variation in the last example, to suggest that fidelity to the original stage-directions should not be expected in Crane transcripts. Indeed, the consistent evidence of the later transcripts is that they were 'improved' for reading. Bald supplies a list of similar directions in Demetrius compared with The Humourous Lieutenant of the Beaumont and Fletcher Folio of 1647; it is not necessary to repeat it here.^{32} Comparison of some stage-directions of Game Folger, his earliest Game transcript, with those of Middleton's Trinity transcript further adds to the impression of the licence Crane allowed himself. These directions have features for which no warrant can be found in the texts related to Middleton's copies, the Bridgewater transcript and Q1 and Q2.

TRINITY

FOLGER

Ind. Ignatius Loyola appearing, Error | at his foote as asleepe.

Ignatius discovered; and Error, a-sleepe.

3.1.165 Enter Bl. Bishop | and both the houses

Enter | Bl. B^p. & | the wh. House. & | Bl. House.

4.1. Enter Bl. Kts pawne meeting the black B^S | pawne richlie accoultred.

...Enter Bl. K^{ts} Pawne, & Bl. B^S. Pawne.

4.3 Enter Bl. queenes pawne as | conducting the White to a | chamber, then fetching in | the Bl. Bishops pawne the | Jesuite conuayes him |

Musick. | Enter Bl. Q^S. P. wth Lights, conducting wh. Q^S Pawne | to a Chamber: and then $\overset{e}{y}$ Bl. B^{ps}. Pawne to an other, & Ex[it]

TRINITY	FOLGER
another puts out the light | and shee followes.	
5.1.40 Musique an Altar discouer^d and Statues, wth a Song	Musick | An Altar disco= -uerd, richely adorned, | and diuers Statues | standing on each-side.

These examples show that stage-directions in Crane transcripts must be used with caution as evidence of the character of the manuscript which he might have had as copy. Crane not only embellished stage-directions with additional details, he also shortened them. There is little evidence that he omitted directions: indeed his tendency was to insert matter which might assist a reader. Game Folger, for instance, has seven exits and two entrances which are not in the Trinity transcript, and, according to Bald's collation, do not appear in the Bridgewater copy or the first two quartos. Some of them occur in Lansdowne and other copies associated with Crane. Therefore, Greg was probably wrong to suggest that 'Crane may have overlooked' the exits and entrances which he noted were missing from Witch.[33] The evidence for the assumption that Crane's transcript was made from the prompt-book is slight, and it is not likely that he would have had access to it in order to make a presentation copy.

One feature of Crane's stage-directions which Greg used to support his study of Witch was entrances which were 'usually, though not always, marked a line or two early'.[34] The Malone Society editors of <u>Demetrius</u> observed that directions in <u>Game</u> Folger and Lansdowne are frequently indicated earlier than the directions in Middleton's Trinity manuscript, and that this may be 'no more than a scribal habit'.[35] These directions are not the anticipatory directions which the book-keeper might insert to ensure that stage properties and special effects would be ready when required: Crane's transcripts contain no examples of such directions. It is the position of ordinary directions in relation to the text which has caused these comments. It should be remarked, therefore, that some of the directions in the <u>Game</u> transcripts vary in position from one copy to the other and, indeed, some occur later than those in Middleton's Trinity manuscript. Three examples of later directions may be seen in the Folger transcript at 1.1.340, 4.4.60 and 5.3.181. One cannot attach much significance to this feature of his transcripts, therefore, although it is interesting to enquire how variation of the placing of directions arose, especially if it casts light on his usual method of copying manuscripts.

It seems that the scribe wrote in the main headings and side directions after the main text had been written, although whether he did this page by page or after he had finished the whole text is not clear. To write the directions for a page at a time appears to be the more natural method but it would not be surprising to find that his practice was not consistent: he might have varied his practice from manuscript to manuscript, or between parts of manuscripts, without its being in our power to distinguish. Dover Wilson thought that 'the additional directions were <u>added</u> to the Lansdowne MS, possibly after the whole dialogue had been transcribed, but more probably as each page was finished'.[36]

In the <u>Game</u> transcripts there is little indication that the dialogue was arranged to allow for the later insertion of side directions, or that lines were broken because a direction which had already been written did not permit the scribe to continue the text on one line. Possibly a stage-direction on p. 92 of <u>Game</u> Folger shows this where 5.3.184, '<u>wh. King</u>. Oh let me blesse mine Armes with this deere Treasure' seems to have been split after 'with' on account of a side stage-direction of three lines which started above. But because the dialogue would have read smoothly without the following words, and because the style of handwriting suggests that they could have been written as an after-thought (perhaps Crane's eye noticed the omission when he was writing the direction separately), this is not conclusive. Further, on p. 21 of the same transcript at l. 339f. the line ends '... the ---'; apparently the dash was used to separate the dialogue from a two-line side direction which prevented Crane from continuing; the text is completed on the following line.

On the other hand there are many directions throughout his transcripts which have been started between the lines of the dialogue or otherwise accommodated to it. This supports the view that they were written after the main text.[37] Simple 'exit's and 'exeunt's written in his informal italic hand were introduced by short dashes which, unlike the heavier dash which usually introduced the main marginal directions, are normally on the line: these directions were clearly written at the same time as the dialogue. More suggestive is a misplaced direction at 5.3.181 (on the same page as an earlier instance) where 'Flourish' was written opposite a line which ends with 'all'. It should correctly appear at 1. 178 which also ends with 'all'. This mistake, it seems, could be explained only if the scribe had returned to the text to write in the side directions separately. It also shows how this scribal practice might affect the text.

SPEECH-PREFIXES

It is conceivable that the speech-prefixes, which were always written in italic, were also added after the dialogue had been written. The speech-prefixes in Barnavelt certainly give that impression from their position in relation to the lines of dialogue. The left-hand column of four into which Crane folded his paper afforded ample space, and he would have been assisted by the speech-rules, which are found in this transcript only. However, it is not necessary to conclude from the absence of rules in the other transcripts that the speech-prefixes there were not separately written, for speech-rules would be intrusive in literary transcripts, and in their absence the scribe's copy would instruct him where to place the speech-prefixes correctly. He did not use a separate wide column for speech-prefixes in the literary transcripts where, although the speech-prefixes are written flush with the left-hand margin and the lines of dialogue are indented somewhat, the longer speech-prefixes like '1 Gent. V.' in Demetrius extend into the body of the text. He usually followed the prefix with a space of about two letters' width but brought following lines of the speech out to the left again to make a text margin distinct from the speech-prefix margin. The disposition of the speech-prefixes and dialogue is neat in Demetrius and Witch but tended to become ragged in the Game transcripts which do not seem to have been given the same careful attention to details of presentation.

Crane usually took no account of stage-directions, act and scene headings and speech-prefixes in the catchwords of his later transcripts: for example, the catchword on p. 33 of the Folger transcript reads 'Is', but the next page starts with a three line stage-direction and 'wh.Q. Is...'. If the catchwords were supplied to assist the correct collation of the manuscript rather than as a superfluous and imitative flourish (since the pages of most of his transcripts are numbered), speech-prefixes in the catchwords would not be helpful. On the other hand, if stage-directions and speech-prefixes were written after the dialogue, catchwords which ignored them might have assisted him to keep the text in proper sequence. It is difficult to see what advantage he might have expected from this practice, save the opportunity to use a different pen in order to improve the appearance of the italic speech-prefixes. There is no evidence that the other words in italic in the dialogue were written separately or with a different pen. Indeed, at 2.1 after the letter to the Black Bishop's Pawn in Game Folger, the scribe incorrectly continued to write in the Italian hand: he reverted to secretary after the first two words of the line. In the same transcript, at 2.2.233, there is little space between 'wh.Kings P.' and 'how' with which the line begins, but usually, as might be expected, the spacing is comfortable. Confusion of speech-prefixes such as the transposition of 'Bl.Kt.' and 'Bl.King' at 3.1.318-19 seems more significant but it need not have arisen from the later addition of speech-prefixes. All in all, the evidence hardly proves that he wrote the speech-prefixes after the dialogue, and it is not likely.[38]

The speech-prefixes in his literary transcripts confirm McKerrow's observations about the regularity and brevity of speech-prefixes in transcripts in general.[39] The Game transcripts supply the most information: the three Crane transcripts and the Trinity manuscript in Middleton's hand are all copies of copies. In the Folger transcript, the earliest Crane transcript, the speech-prefixes are short but there are some alternative forms in different passages of the text. Two examples are 'Bl. B/Bl.Bp.' for Black Bishop, and 'Wh.Bps.P./Wh.Bsh.P./ Wh.Bs.P.' for White Bishop's Pawn. In Game Lansdowne and Game Malone, which were copied from the same, lost, transcript, the speech-prefixes are shorter: hence, prefixes like 'Bl.B., Bl.Kt., Bl.P.' and 'Bl.Q.' are usually the only forms by which the respective characters are designated. When there are alternative forms, the short speech-prefixes are much more frequent than the longer. There is little to be learned from the speech-prefixes in these transcripts, although it might be useful to observe that Crane did not favour extreme contraction of speakers' names. 'B.B.' for Black Bishop, and similar contractions, do not occur in his transcripts, although they are to be found in Q3 which was printed from a transcript of his which has not survived. The number of speech-prefix variants there is so great, however, that the compositors must have been very influential on the forms of speech-prefixes.

In Barnavelt he can be seen casting around for a settled form of speech-prefix. On f. 18 for instance, after the stage-direction 'Enter Modes-bargen | & Huntesman', the speech-prefixes run 'Modesb.', '1.Huntes.', 'Mod.' and '2.Hunt.' as Crane fixes on acceptable abbreviations for the names of characters he has not encountered for some time. Once he had transcribed Game for the first time, however, the speech-prefixes must have been quite fixed in his mind. Nor are there instances of that variation in which a character is represented by his function or some other epithet rather than by name, as in Henry V, for example, where 'Fluellen' and 'Iamy' become 'Welch.' and 'Scot.'. There is greater variety of speech-prefixes in Barnavelt as might be expected in a transcript close to the authors' papers, but they do not correspond to the division of the text between Fletcher and Massinger. In short, the speech-prefixes in Crane's transcripts are usually concise, and he generally uses one style consistently. The speech-prefixes become more regular as he transcribes and retranscribes a text.

Crane's use of italics in the dialogue is not remarkable. Stage-directions, speech-prefixes, act and scene headings, songs and letters were conventionally italicised,

and he often italicised the first word of an act or scene
as an embellishment. Proper nouns and sometimes other
nouns like '<u>Prince</u>, <u>King</u>' and '<u>Leiuetenant</u>', in <u>Demetrius</u>,
and abstract nouns like '<u>Honor</u>' and '<u>Vertue</u>' were fairly
consistently emphasised with italics, and occasionally,
as the same text shows, there are short passages where a
character in the play reads from a book or a letter which
are distinguished from the context by being written in the
Italian hand. It was sometimes employed with capital
letters for special emphasis, as in line 1.1.34 of <u>Game</u>
Folger: 'And here come <u>He</u>, whose sanctimonious Breath...',
and sometimes in place of quotation marks for sententia
or proverbs. There appear to be relatively more words
emphasised by italics in the 'literary' later transcripts
than in transcripts made for performance such as <u>Barnavelt</u>.

PUNCTUATION MARKS

Two tables which show how frequently marks of
punctuation occur in Crane's transcripts are set out on
the following page. The first gives counts of punctuation
which were obtained by a computer program, and beneath it
is a table of proportional figures obtained by dividing
the counts into the number of words in the text. The
table of proportions overcomes to some extent the
difficulty of comparing the raw counts for marks of
punctuation of texts of different lengths. In this table,
the smaller the proportional figure, the greater is the
frequency of the mark of punctuation in that text. It
need hardly be mentioned that the extent of the inferences
which can be made from these figures is limited by the
simplicity of the statistical treatment supplied by the

MARKS OF PUNCTUATION IN CRANE TRANSCRIPTS

TEXT	DATE	.	?	!	:	;	,	( )	'	-[1]	Caps.	Words	Total
PRV	'18	83	45	0	72	20	263	14	40	12	158	2536	707
Bar.	'19	561	308	5	750	143	2230	121	390	47	1327	23067	5882
GmF.	'24	548	276	0	430	104	1272	184	650	389	2621	16180	6475
GmL.	'24	558	342	0	639	114	1493	356	669	360	3258	18256	7789
GmM.	'24/5	523	227	0	353	43	825	258	391	341	2476	12427	5437
Wit.	'24/5	618	252	0	548	182	1341	198	877	362	1846	17345	6224
Dem.	'25	672	685	0	1615	331	2138	480	871	175	1990	26299	9057
Ded.	'25-32	92	1	0	76	35	301	99	44	80	615	3039	1343

PROPORTION OF PUNCTUATION TO NUMBER OF WORDS IN TEXT

TEXT	DATE	.	?	!	:	;	,	( )	'	-[1]	Caps.	Words	Rel. density.
PRV	'18	30	56	-	35	127	9	181	63	211	15	2536	3.6
Bar.	'19	41	75	-	30	161	10	268	59	49	16	23067	3.9
GmF.	'24	29	59	-	39	155	12	88	25	41	6	16180	2.5
GmL.	'24	32	53	-	28	160	12	51	28	50	5	18256	2.4
GmM.	'24/5	23	54	-	35	289	15	48	31	36	5	12427	2.3
Wit.	'24/5	28	69	-	31	95	13	87	19	48	9	17345	2.8
Dem.	'25	39	38	-	16	79	12	55	30	150	13	26299	2.9
Ded.	'25-32	33	-	-	39	86	10	30	69	38	5	3039	2.3

1. Hyphens. Full stops after speech-prefixes and contractions such as L. for 'Lord', and in acronyms, and capitals beginning lines, after full stops, question and exclamation marks, and in words all in capitals, are not included in the counts. The figures for 'Relative density' have been rounded.

tables. The column 'Relative density' gives the result of dividing the total punctuation counts of a text into the number of words. The figures in this column show clearly that the later transcripts are more heavily punctuated than the earlier, a characteristic which is confirmed by the figure for the dedications of 1625-32. This 'text' includes Crane's dedications from <u>Demetrius</u> (1625) to <u>The Faulty Favorite</u> (1632), and his holographic <u>Summary</u> (1626), and supplies some evidence of his formal punctuation when he was not influenced by copy. <u>Demetrius</u> appears to be exceptional to the general observation that punctuation became more frequent in his transcripts over the years; the low number of hyphens has obscured the true relationship of <u>Witch</u> and <u>Demetrius</u>. When allowance is made for this, <u>Demetrius</u> is slightly more densely punctuated overall than <u>Witch</u>.

The general tendency for the punctuation to increase is sometimes obscured when one mark of punctuation is preferred to another. There is obviously a close relationship between the incidence of full stops and marks of interrogation, and amongst the lesser stops, colons, semicolons, and commas. Parentheses and commas are also related when they were used to mark off vocatives. There is little variation in Crane's use of full stops, colons, commas and capitals, particularly in the later transcripts. The proportions of apostrophes, however, vary considerably; in the <u>Game</u> transcripts at least, this may be partly explained by his practice of omitting apostrophes in Jonsonian elisions. As the dedications are mainly prose, the low proportion of apostrophes there is not remarkable. In general, the tendency to more elaborate punctuation is clear: where some figures appear to be anomalous, they can usually be explained by making some allowance for the particular character of the transcript in question.

Little need be said about Crane's parentheses which have often been cited as evidence of his influence on a text, for I have discussed their occurrence in texts associated with him in detail elsewhere.[40] My conclusion about the parentheses in transcripts should however be recorded here:

> Although there are relatively few parentheses in Crane's own manuscripts, they are proportionally more frequent than in his dramatic transcripts; however, he did not prefer vocative parentheses. (2) The dramatic transcripts made between 1618 and 1622, all non-literary texts, reveal a lower proportion of parentheses, especially used vocatively, than the literary texts of 1624-25.
> (3) <u>Lansdowne MS. 690</u>, <u>Malone MS. 25</u>, <u>Demetrius and Enanthe</u>, and <u>London's Visitation</u> are linked by a common proportion of parentheses, which suggests that the last two transcripts are, like the first two, Crane transcripts from his own earlier copy.[41]

A reviewer commented that I should have considered the vocative parentheses in relation to the number of vocative constructions in the transcripts before concluding that non-vocative rather than vocative parentheses were more characteristic of Crane.[42] It would be unnecessarily onerous to identify all the vocatives but perhaps a selection of words which occur more often as vocatives would show whether he preferred to mark them off with parentheses as the conventional opinion holds. In the dramatic transcripts at least, such words as 'Sir', 'S^r', 'Sirha',

'Madam' and 'Lady' are frequently vocatives and occur often enough to supply a reliable index to his practice. The figures for the texts in chronological order, with the percentage of vocatives in parentheses, are: Barnavelt 111 (0%); Game Folger 115 (27%); Game Lansdowne 112 (83%); Game Malone 91 (90%); Witch 173 (34%); and Demetrius 231 (78%). These figures confirm the earlier conclusion: the texts in which vocatives without parentheses predominate are (with the exception of Demetrius) those which he transcribed from author's copy. Demetrius, as has been suggested, seems to be more like Game Lansdowne and Malone, and this could be used with other evidence to show that it too was Crane's transcript of his own earlier copy.

It is doubtful in any case, since it was not difficult for a scribe or compositor to pick out the forms of address in their copy which could be given parentheses, that vocative parentheses could be very useful as evidence of the character of the original copy. On the other hand, Crane's other parentheses show attention to the syntax of the text which was not as likely to be given by a compositor in the usual course of events. However, it is not impossible that he became addicted to vocative parentheses over the years and that the relatively lower proportions of Witch and Demetrius, which were probably transcribed within months of each other, are not significant. Nevertheless, these figures give little support to the view that a high number of vocative parentheses is a sure indication of his influence on texts prepared before 1624. They might show up, however, in a text printed from a transcript of his own papers: <u>WT</u>, as will be seen later, might be an example of such a text.

Capitalisation in his transcripts follows the pattern of the punctuation, becoming more frequent over the years, especially in texts which he copied from his own transcripts. He seems to have followed his own inclination in <u>Game</u> Folger because Middleton's manuscript, as <u>Game</u> Trinity shows, has relatively few capitalised words. He made no rule about the beginning of lines of verse: if they start with capitals it is generally because the first word was a noun or adjective which he would ordinarily have capitalised, but not infrequently he would capitalise pronouns or verbs. Partridge is not correct when he writes that Crane frequently capitalised pronouns and the relative 'that'.[43] Of the 1748 times 'that' occurs in the dramatic transcripts, only 27 have capitals, and some of these are at the beginning of lines or sentences. Relatively more 'she's and 'we's appear to be capitalised, but Crane's initial 's' and 'w' are ambiguous, and not too much can be made of the evidence.

Sometimes compositors found it difficult to distinguish prose from verse if the verse lines did not start with capitals in their copy. Often it cannot be decided whether Crane realised that he was transcribing verse because he did not extend lines of prose uniformly to the right-hand margins of his transcripts. <u>Witch</u> gives two good examples of this on facing pages at 1. 279-85 and 297-301: the Malone Society reprint shows the relation of verse and prose sufficiently well for comparison. In other passages which Bullen prints as prose there is no perceptible difference between the arrangement of prose and verse lines in the transcript.[44] Middleton's verse in Game Trinity sprawls across the page to the right-hand margin so that Crane would not have had an easy task to distinguish the prose passages had he wished to. The Game transcripts supply little information about Crane's ability to identify prose in his copy. Lines 5.3.205-9 are written as prose in Middleton's manuscript but as verse in Crane's Lansdowne transcript, but as it is possible that the lineation was correct as verse in the manuscript from which he made this transcript, this is no evidence of his ability to distinguish between prose and verse. At 4.2 where the Black Knight reads the prices from 'the Booke of generall pardons', the prose lines are written in italic in all Crane's transcripts, but his copy was quite clear.

More significantly, apart from the passages of prose which Crane wrote in italics, he gave no guide to compositors or editors. J. R. Brown notes that most of the prose in The Duchess of Malfi, which he finds to have been printed from a Crane transcript, is arranged in lines which have capitals at the beginning but do not extend to the full width of the compositor's measure.[45] It would not be surprising to find similar passages in other texts set from Crane transcripts, especially if the metre was so irregular that the distinction between prose and verse was not easily perceivable.

Game Folger probably shows the density of punctuation which might be expected in any transcript he made for the Folio, but the style of his pointing is probably best

studied in the more lavishly punctuated Demetrius. It
would be hazardous, however, to compare this with The
Humourous Lieutenant where compositors would have had
much influence, so once again Game Trinity must be used
in order to study the punctuation Crane added to his
copy (on the presumption that the Middleton manuscript
from which he transcribed Game Folger was pointed in
similar fashion). The first two scenes of the fifth act
have 170 lines in common in Bald's edition. Crane
added 82 marks of punctuation and omitted 20: the
addition and omission of commas made up approximately half
of each figure. Significant additional punctuation were
9 hyphens and 9 apostrophes, and 10 full stops at the end
of sentences. Very often Middleton used a light stop at
the end of a sentence for which Crane almost invariably
substituted a heavier. The most significant variation is
between commas, and colons, which Crane preferred on 27
occasions. All the changed punctuation save the omissions
and additions, and 7 occurrences of the substitution for
a punctuation mark by one of equivalent weight, supply
heavier stops. There are 76 heavier stops in all, of
which 27 are commas changed to colons.

    The character of the punctuation apart from this is
not exceptional. Middleton's punctuation was not lavish
and a modern editor would follow Crane in many of his
alterations.[46] I have noticed no peculiarities of
practice which might serve to identify his influence in
printed texts.[47] However, an editor, especially if there
were grounds for believing that Crane's copy was not
heavily punctuated, would be justified in regarding commas
and colons, which are relatively frequent in his tran-

scripts, as of little authority. It would be surprising if there is much of Fletcher's punctuation, for example, in such a line as l. 927 of <u>Barnavelt</u>: 'all o^r designes are crackt, layed open; ruynd:'. The parentheses too, and not only those around vocatives, and hyphens, and many of the more meticulous instances of the use of apostrophes, probably owe more to the scribe than his copy.

HYPHENATION

The Malone Society editors have discussed his contractions, hyphenated-compounds and elisions so fully that there is little need for more here than a summary account of Crane's peculiarities. The interest of his orthography and the extent of the detailed tabulated information provided by the concordances of his transcripts tempt one to write at length on matters which have already been discussed by recent writers on Crane. However, it does not seem necessary to go over this ground again and I shall discuss in greater detail only those features of Crane's orthography which may have affected the text of manuscripts which he transcribed.

As the table of punctuation shows, the number of hyphenated-compounds varies considerably: the 12 in Jonson's <u>Pleasure</u> include none of the verb/preposition compounds which are usually taken to be characteristic of Crane, and the two occurences of verb/pronoun compounds ('come-it' and 'some-it') are metrical compounds at the ends of verse lines which he probably reproduced from copy. <u>Barnavelt</u> with 29 hyphenated-compounds gives

no examples of these varieties and it would not be
surprising if he had followed the hyphenation of his copy
in this transcript quite closely. In common with other
marks of punctuation, hyphens became increasingly
frequent in his later transcripts and the dedications
show that by 1626 he was addicted to their use.

Greg discussed five kinds of hyphenation in his
Malone Society reprint of Witch which draws largely on his
earlier paper on this text.[48] Some further types of
compound can be added to these in order to define Crane's
practice more precisely. Greg noticed the adverb and
adjective ('truelie-ennobled' in the dedications),
adjective(s) and substantive ('humblest-deuoted-beades-
man' in the dedications), and the compounding of a common
prefix with a stem, as in 'be-thinck' in the dedications.
These are common to all his transcripts and are not
uncommon in printed texts. Greg distinguished two verb
compounds, one in which a dependent preposition or adverb
is compounded: 'came-in' is an instance from the
dedications; this kind of hyphenated-compound is too
frequent for it to be necessary to add to the examples in
Greg's article. Hyphenation of verb and pronoun is less
common and may be a surer indication of Crane's influence.
Examples of this in the transcripts, in chronological
order, are: Pleasure 'come-it', 'some-it', perhaps from
copy; Game Folger 'hugg-thee, pree-thee, pre-thee'; Game
Lansdowne 'pree-thee, pre-thee, produce-him, whip-you';
Game Malone 'hug-thee, milkd-her, saincted-me, vndoe-him,
wynn-thee'; Witch 'box-me, clapd-it, hye-thee, pitty-me,
pree-thee, pre-thee'; Demetrius 'buoy-her, sett-me, wynn-
her', and in the dedications, 'continew-you'.[49]

Occasionally he hyphenates the indefinite article with following words, as in the three <u>Game</u> transcripts, 'a-day'; <u>Witch</u> 'a-hundred, with-a-ioy'; <u>Demetrius</u> 'a-devill', and in the dedications, 'a-readie-writer' and 'a-worke'. Hyphenation of a possessive with a following substantive is fairly frequent, sometimes with the possessive apostrophe as in 'vertue's-sake' in <u>Game</u> Folger and 'Christ's-yoake' in the dedications, and sometimes with loss or assimilation of the inflexional 's' as in 'heaven-sake' in <u>Barnavelt</u> and 'trust-sake' in <u>Game</u> Malone. He is not consistent in these practices, as 'vertues-sake' in <u>Game</u> Lansdowne shows. Some adverbs or relative pronouns are liable to be hyphenated: 'some-what' in <u>Witch</u> and the dedications is an instance. Other words of this kind are 'how-ere, soe-ere, some-what, some-other, oft-times, far-off, what-ever', and 'some-where'. He is apt to hyphenate adjectives and pronouns of the type 'brave-ones, sure-one' and 'self-same' in <u>Game</u> Folger and Malone, and inverted substantives and adjectives such as 'hope-monarchall' in <u>Game</u> Folger. There are some compounded intensifying adjectives and adverbs such as 'too-too' (in 'too-too many disasters, too-too much weakend my ...' in the dedications), 'too-much, no-other, so-long, so-much, too-low, yet-ever' and 'even-off', but there is only one instance of a preposition joined to a pronoun: 'ore-me' in <u>Demetrius</u>. In <u>Witch</u> and <u>Demetrius</u> some vocatives are hyphenated: 'how-now, y-faith, by'r-lady' and 'god-a-mercy', and there are a few instances of pronouns with following adverbs or pronouns: "'em-me, me-that" in <u>Game</u> Folger; 'you-ward' in <u>Game</u> Lansdowne and Malone, and "'em-off" in <u>Demetrius</u>. Pronouns are hyphenated with substantives in 'she' compounds such as 'she-frend' in the <u>Game</u> transcripts; 'that-blessed-spring' in <u>Game</u> Folger is a more elaborate compound of this kind. Occasionally he compounds a substantive with a following adverb as in 'capon-like' in the <u>Game</u> transcripts, and 'fate-on, frog-too' and 'life-blood-in' in the <u>Witch</u>. The only occurrence of a verb compounded with a following auxiliary is 'hast-not' in <u>Witch</u>. Hyphenation of reflexive pronouns is rare: 'my-self' in <u>Game</u> Lansdowne and 'her-self' and 'our-self' in <u>Witch</u> are the only instances. There are a few hyphenated prepositions and substantives: 'on-conscience' and 'o'-life' in <u>Game</u> Lansdowne and Malone, 'after-thanckes-giving' in <u>Game</u> Malone, 'in-troth' in <u>Witch</u>, and two examples of a verb hyphenated with a substantive: 'take-place' in <u>Game</u> Folger and Malone, and 'make-way' in <u>Game</u> Malone and <u>Witch</u>.

Hyphenation increases in the transcripts both in frequency and in the variety of use, from <u>Pleasure</u> to his dedications: when he came to compose his dedications, he used hyphens as a matter of course. However, he was not consistent in using them for all constructions of the kind mentioned above, or in reproducing the hyphens which were present in his copy. It seems too that four of the five categories Greg distinguished are too frequent amongst printed texts of the period to be significant evidence of Crane's influence, and it may be, as will be seen when I examine the Folio comedies, that the less common kinds of hyphenation give more reliable evidence of his influence on a text.

Many of the orthographical changes Crane made to his copy were intended to assist readers: his orthography

SCRIBAL PRACTICES IN TRANSCRIPTS   43

tended toward greater formality over the years.
Consequently, conventional and common scribal contractions such as 'w^{ch}', 'wth', and 'y^{e}' are rarer in his
transcripts than might have been expected from a scribe
with his experience of legal and commercial transcription.
His Rejoinder has many different contractions of
'complaint' and 'complainant', and of 'defendant', but
few other contractions. Possibly he inclined by nature
to a formal sort of writing. There are 29 'w^{ch}'s in
Barnavelt, 12 in Pleasure, but not half this number in
the rest of his transcripts together. Similarly, 'S^{r}',
occurs 37 times in Barnavelt but never again in dialogue.
Pleasure is exceptional for 'y^{ei}, y^{eir}, y^{eis}, y^{em}, y^{em}selues'
and 'y^{m}selues', and for many ampersands in the dialogue:
thereafter ampersands are found almost without exception
only in stage-directions and act and scene headings.
Indeed, contractions in the transcripts after Pleasure
are limited to stage-directions and the superscriptions
of his dedications. Contractions such as 'l.' for 'Lord'
and 'S.' for 'Saint' are rare: 'S^{t}' occurs once each in
Barnavelt and Game Lansdowne. Numerous contractions are
not characteristic of Crane's transcripts and it is fairly
certain that when they are found in texts printed from
his transcripts, compositors were responsible.

APOSTROPHES AND ELISIONS

On the other hand, he used apostrophes lavishly to
indicate elision, and the omission, sometimes notional,
of letters in such words as 'has't' and 'bee'st'. Of the
many different kinds of elision which are found in his
transcripts the most important for an editor are those

which affect the metre or those which, because of his carelessness in positioning the apostrophe, a compositor might have misread. Very often, as the Game transcripts show, he used different forms of elision in transcripts of the same text. Hence, one encounters these variants in his transcripts: "I'am/I'me; they're/wee're/you're/ we'ar/y'ar/you'ar/they'are/they'r/we'are/y'are/ye'are/ you'are; art'/art'not/art'thou/thou'rt/thou'art; they'de/haue'had/it'had/he'had/I'had/'t'had/they'had/ you'had; h'as/ha's/'has/has/h'has/'ithas/it'has; hast'it/ thou'hast/thou'st; 't'hath/hath/'hath/h'ath/hath'; ha'/ I'ha/I'haue/I'ue/haue'byn/they'haue/they'ue/y'aue/you'haue/ ye'haue/y'haue; ile/I'll/hee'll/he'll/she'll/shee'll/ they'll/wee'll/you'll; hee'll'd/Ill'd/I'would/she'll'd/ she'would/they'll'd/they'would/you'ld/you'll'd/you'would". (Middleton preferred 'I'me, 're, 'rt, 'de, 'ue, 'll and 'll'd'.)

It is interesting that the elisions that Greg called 'Jonsonian' (although they can be found from earliest times),[50] where an apostrophe is used to indicate the elision of syllables although the full spellings are retained, are most certainly Crane's 'improvements'. Their frequency, in summary, is: Pleasure 1 ('by'vn-altered', 1. 188), Barnavelt 1 ('the'Arminians', 1. 587), Game Folger 16, Game Lansdowne 45, Game Malone 8, Witch 52, and Demetrius 14.[51] The surprisingly low figure for Game Malone can be explained by another characteristic of Crane's treatment of elisions which is discussed later. It seems, then, that Jonsonian elisions are a good indication of his influence on a text.

Some other contractions and spellings with which he used apostrophes may also provide helpful evidence of his habits. There are several examples of his use of the apostrophe to denote the omission of a common word, a pronoun or an article perhaps, as in "'has" or "'hath" for '[he] has' or '[he] hath', "beleeue'" (<u>Demetrius</u> l. 471), "'pray" (<u>Demetrius</u> l. 3300), "at'back-dore" (<u>Witch</u> l. 1049) "at'lower-end" (<u>Game</u> Lansdowne l. 2394). The "at clensing of the pond" of <u>Game</u> Lansdowne (l. 2440) becomes "at' clensing ..." in the Malone transcript. He usually used apostrophes to indicate the loss of a short unaccented initial vowel or syllable in "'boue, 'bout, 'cause, 'gainst, 'mongst, 'stead, 'tweene" and "'twixt", for example, but not every such aphetic or apheretic elision was given an apostrophe. Generally, however, it is rare to find the familiar contractions "and't, at's, do'em, do't, don't, doo't, 'em, er't, eu'n, eu'r, for't, he's, into't, let's, neu'r, on's, 'twas, 'twer, 'twere, 'twilbe, 'twill, 'twould" and the frequent 'is' and 'it' elisions without apostrophes, even though he might vary its position in such elisions as "i'th'". His usual form was "i'th'", which occurs 55 times; there are only 5 occurrences of "i'th". <u>Barnavelt</u> is exceptional with 6 occurrences of "ith'", 3 of "oth'", 9 of "h'as" or "ha's" for "'has", and 37 "ile" spellings, which are rare in other transcripts.[52] The use of apostrophes in "oth" is similar: 27 "o'th'" and 5 "o'th", but "to'th'" offers little useful information: "toth" occurs 5 times (3 in <u>Barnavelt</u>), "to'th'" and "to'th" once each in different transcripts. "Th'" almost always has the apostrophe.

The compound verb auxiliaries are interesting.
'Shalbe' occurs 41 times in <u>Barnavelt</u>, the <u>Game</u> transcripts, <u>Witch</u>, and <u>Demetrius</u>, but 'shall be' only 5 times. "'twilbe, wilbe, 'twas" and "'twould" are common, but as they are also found in <u>Game</u> Trinity, the spellings are not significant. However, 'shalbe' and 'wilbe' together occur 9 times in <u>Game</u> Folger; in each case Middleton's Trinity transcript has the full form. An editor can be fairly confident that, although compositors commonly used 'shalbe' and 'wilbe' (sometimes for justification), a good proportion of them will be Crane's in any text printed from his transcripts.

Crane was not consistent in the use of the apostrophe to show syncope of non-syllabic '-ed'. In <u>Game</u> Folger, in words from A to D inclusive, there are 19 apostrophes, but 54 occasions on which the apostrophe was omitted; there is about the same proportion of <u>Game</u> Lansdowne where he was not influenced by the habit of the author. Other examples of syncope show much the same habit: although he sometimes used the apostrophe in words like 'diffring' and 'veng'aunce', he had no consistent practice, as 'venison' (<u>Barnavelt</u> 1. 2823), 'venson' (<u>Witch</u> 1. 79) and 'ven'son' (<u>Demetrius</u> 1. 119) demonstrate, and it is doubtful whether apostrophes in similar words can be used to show his influence on a text. He made greater use of the apostrophe with possessives but again, he is not consistent. More significant perhaps, is that he did not restrict these to possessive proper nouns of romance origin. 'Christ's-yoake, God's-mercie, heaven's' and 'world's-troubles' occur in the dedications, and the earlier dramatic transcripts have many occurrences of 'bishop's' and 'queene's'. 'Angell's, Diall's, Confessor's, it's, Vertue's, Honor's, Truthe's, Miller's' and 'Lust's' are some further examples from Game Folger.

METRE

Amongst the elisions already mentioned are some which may be significant for the metre of texts Crane transcribed. Perhaps it is most important to decide whether he had any regard at all for the proper representation of metrical values, whether he tampered with the metre of his copy, and how much his practices might have influenced texts printed from his transcripts. As before, the Game transcripts supply convenient means for the examination of these questions. For convenience I have tabulated the metrical variants in the first three acts of Game. A blank in a column signifies that the reading of that transcript is substantially that of the preceding column; a dash means that the line is not found in that transcript.

VARIANTS OF POTENTIAL INFLUENCE ON THE METRE IN 'GAME', ACTS 1-3

Line No.	Trinity (M)	Folger	Lansdowne	Malone
Ind.				
6	theyde...ouer		they'had	
18	they had			they'had
30	twentieth	twentith		
45	to it	to't		
49	mastrie	mastery		
59	theire	they're	They are	
70	I'de haue had	Ill'd haue had	I'would haue' had	I'would haue had

48   CRANE AND SOME FOLIO COMEDIES

Line No.	Trinity (M)	Folger	Lansdowne	Malone
74	haue'em		haue them	
77	you'de	you'll'd	you'would	you'ld
80	See'em...marke'em			See them...marke them
1.1.				
1	ne're		never	
8	they're		Theis are	
27	e'en		euen	
45	e'en		euen	
55	they're		They are	---
57	the Vniuersall	th'Vniversall	the Vniuersall	---
65	to the Father	to th'		---
69	mysterie			
74	do'st finde	doe you		
113	Who is	Who's		
148	They'de	they'had		they had
188	redeeme them	'em		
199	I haue	I'haue		---
210	I haue	I'haue		I haue
222	I marrie her		I'would	
232	haue I bin		I'haue byn	I haue byn
239	unhallowed ['d]			
242	They're		they'are	
245	t'infect		to infect	
274	I'ue	I haue	I'haue	I haue
275	But haue	I'haue		
278	I haue...I haue	I haue...I ha'	I'haue...I'haue	I haue...I haue
284	sugred	sugard		
312	youde	you'll'd	you'ld	
313	weere		we'are	we are
323	of the black	o'th'	of the	
326	the Assistant	th'		
330	Thinke theyue	'thinck they'ue	they'haue	I thinck they haue

SCRIBAL PRACTICES IN TRANSCRIPTS 49

Line No.	Trinity (M)	Folger	Lansdowne	Malone
332	They put	they'ue	they'haue	they'haue
337	Er't		ere it	
339	Though it	though't	though it	
341	weere		we'are	we are
343	hearts			hart is
360	thou'rt		thou'art	
2.1.				
35	I haue		I'haue	
69	by it	by't		---
77	to the house	to th'		---
130	carrie it	carry't		---
132	Thou'rt		Thou art	---
133	to it	to't		---
157	to undoo	t'vndooe		---
162	I uenture	I'll		---
165	in the Conuocation	i'th'		---
170	the Alarum	th'		---
176	of the whitehouse	o'th'		---
181	youre	y'ar		---
184	y'aue	y'haue	you'haue	---
242	see it	see't	see it	
252	scortch mee'em	scortch'em me		
258	spectacld	spectacled		
259	of the Dung	o'th'	of the	---
274	to the Ground	to th'		---
2.2.				
14	Agaynst		'gainst	---
43	I'ue		I'haue	---
118	sufferings	suffrings		
123	of the Vniuersall	o'th'		
173	they'de	they'll'd	---	---
177	the forenamde	the aforenamd	th'aforenam'd	---
204	i'th end		in th'end	
223	They'ue		they'haue	
244	To it		to't	---
254	the offence	th'offence	the Offence	---
279	'tad	't'had	it had	---
282	Youre		You are	
3.1.				
6	where's		where is	---
7	Ide haue		I'would haue	---
47	receiude		receiued	---
56	I'me		I am	---

Line No.	Trinity (M)	Folger	Lansdowne	Malone
73	in the place		i'th'	---
82	Amongst			mongst
96	they haue	they'ue		they' haue
115	in the Ayre			th' Aire
119	I'me	I am	I'am	I am
120	alate		of late	---
148	Twill		it will	---
149	I'me	I am		---
151	They'de		they'had	---
154	twixt		betwixt	
159	the'Assistant	th'assistant		
163	of thc waye	o'th'	of the way	---
184	to expresse	t'expresse	to expresse	---
198	I'me	I am		---
201	I haue		I'haue	---
215	confirmed		confirmd	
223	Shee'de	she'll'd	she'would	She would
275	Ime...to it	I'me...to't	I'am	---
277	Youre		You are	
282	Ide	I'll'd	I would	
285	Doo it	Do't		
286	in this playe	i'this	in this	
291	to the Queene	to th'	to the	
302	raysed	raisd		
314	Ide teare'em	I'll'd	I would teare him	---
344	I'me	---	I am	
358	youle	you'll		
361	thou hast	thou'hast		Thou hast
374	You'le	you'll		
376	thou'rt		thou art	---
378	of his	on's		---
3.2.				
2	Ide	I'll'd	---	---
4	I'de	I'll'd	---	---
7	you would	you'll'd	---	---
10	A pox	'pox	---	---
11	I'me	I am	---	---
18	e're	euer	---	---
21	I'me	I am	---	---
31	I'me	I am	---	---

SCRIBAL PRACTICES IN TRANSCRIPTS   51

Line No.	Trinity (M)	Folger	Lansdowne	Malone
33	of it	on't	---	---
39	I'me	I am	---	---
3,3.				
27	the Imperious	th'Emperious		
72	in the eye	i'th'	in the'ye	---

Variants which Crane substituted for the elisions in Middleton's copy (assuming that Game Trinity represents Middleton's practice) can be disregarded, save that it must be remembered that when Crane expanded elisions with an apostrophe or did not mark the apostrophe clearly or in the proper place, as he sometimes did, compositors could sometimes fail to recognise that an elision was intended. Such lines in printed texts could be hypermetrical. However, there is no need to look more closely at variant elisions which do not affect the metre at Ind.6, 77; 1.1.238 (will be/wilbe), 242, 284, 312; 2.1.181, 184; 2.2.86 (shall be/shalbe), 173, 223; 3.1.7, 47 (prose), 151, 159 (an uncharacteristic Jonsonian elision of Middleton's that may not have been in Crane's copy), 240 (shall bee/shalbe/shall be), 358, 374; 3.2.2., 4; and 3.3.24 (shall bee/ shalbe). There are also many 'Ile/I'll' substitutions which have not been listed. As I have already noted, Jonsonian elisions become more frequent in the later Game transcripts. The table shows this clearly, and shows, moreover, that particularly in the Lansdowne and Malone transcripts which were furtherest removed from authorial copy, expanded forms of elisions frequently lack proper apostrophes.[53] Other readings where Crane substituted an elided for a full form in the text suggest that he recognised their importance for metre, but it is likely that when he prepared a transcript for private reading, he left the reader to infer the appropriate elisions for himself. The omission of apostrophes in elisions in <u>Game</u> Malone especially runs against his increased use of apostrophes in general. Examples of elisions without apostrophes can be seen at Ind.59, 70; 1.1.8, 55, 148, 274, 313, 341; 2.1.132; 2.2.43, 279, 282; 3.1.56, 119, 149, 198, 223, 277, 282, 314, 344, 376; 3.2.11, 21, 31 and 39. Some of these alterations improve the metre but this is adventitious: this cannot have been Crane's intention. On the other hand, there are lines into which he introduced elisions: Ind.18, 45; 1.1.57, 65, 113, 199, 210, 323, 326, 339; 2.1.69, 77, 130, 133, 157, 165, 170, 176, 242, 259, 274; 2.2.123, 244; 3.1.73, 96, 115, 163, 184, 201, 275, 285, 286, 291, 378; 3.2.7, 33; 3.3.27 and 72. Many of these can be regarded as simple formalisations of elisions which a contemporary speaker or reader would have made as a matter of course. When an author used an elided spelling one may be fairly sure that he intended to indicate how the line should be read, but often even in authorial manuscripts there are lines which can be read properly only by introducing elisions which the author had not troubled himself to supply. The view that McKerrow expressed in his <u>Prolegomena</u> seems to fit the facts. He wrote:

> Actually I doubt whether either author or compositor was greatly concerned to assist readers to scan the lines by this means. Shakespeare was writing for actors who were well accustomed to speaking verse, and I cannot but think that he would have expected them to speak his lines as sense and dramatic propriety required without any such adventitious aids as these.[54]

SCRIBAL PRACTICES IN TRANSCRIPTS   53

Little significance can be given to variation of elisions such as those last listed, or to Crane's substitution of the syncopated spelling 'twentith' at Ind.30, the expansion of 'mastrie' at Ind.49, his failure to indicate syncopation in 'mysterie' at 1.1.69 and in 'unhallowed' at 1.1.239, the expansion of 't'infect' at 1.1.245, 'er't' at 1.1.337, 'heart's' at 1.1.343, 'spectacld' at 2.1.258, the syncopation of 'sufferings' at 2.2.118, the introduction or substitution of elisions at 2.2.204 and 254, expansion at 3.1.6 and 148, substitution for '-ed' at 3.1.215 and 302, or even the expansion or reduction of 'em' and 'them' at Ind.74, 80, and 1.1.188[55] and other common contractions at 1.1.1, 27 and 45.[56]

What is important for an editor here is that Crane was not constrained by the representation of metrical values of his copy. The direction of his interference, whether to the benefit or the harm of the metre, is of relatively small moment, for once it is appreciated how far-reaching his influence on orthography was, elisions in texts printed from Crane transcripts cannot be regarded as authoritative, and editors should be vigilant for elisions which have been conflated to the detriment of the metre.

Thus far I have discussed mainly the extent to which Crane followed the forms by which his copy indicated metrical values, whether by elisions or by syncopated spellings. Metre may be affected more seriously however, if a scribe or compositor tampered with the text so that words were introduced to make the syllable count conform

to his notion of metrical regularity. The three instances
of Crane's variation of aphetic contractions, at 2.2.14,
3.1.82 and 154, are not many out of the great number of
such spellings in Game. There are other lines in which
his interference with the metre is potentially more
serious: the authority of these readings is not supported by Bald's collation of the transcripts and quartos
more closely related to Middleton's original manuscript.
Unfortunately, the effect of these variants is ambiguous.
Middleton's blank verse is prosaic, to say the least, and
many lines defeat attempts at scansion even when all
permissible kinds of elision have been tried. A scribe,
like a compositor, would tend to accentuate the base
rhythm as he carried the line in his head during transcription, and it might be expected that even variant
readings which the scribe introduced unconsciously would
tend towards metrical regularity. Readings at 1.1.74,
278 (Lansdowne); 2.2.177 (Lansdowne) lead to a more
satisfying scansion, but at 4.2.43 and 4.4.64, Crane did
not indicate elisions which would have assisted scansion
even though he seems to have been aware that there was
something wrong with the metre. Attempts to make
Middleton's verses conform to strict iambic pentameter
would have required an amount of textual alteration that
even Crane could not bring himself to. Other readings at
1.1.232, 275, 332; 2.1.162, 252; 4.1.171 are corrections
or improvements of what Crane took to have been lapses of
the author; they change the syntax and sometimes the
meaning of Middleton's text. The effect on metre is
negligible save at 4.2.98 which in Game Trinity reads:
"Adulterie? oh I'me in't now,". In Folger this becomes
a regular iambic pentameter.

CRANE'S ACCURACY

It is not necessary to seek evidence of his treatment of metre in other transcripts, for the Game transcripts show clearly that he did not seek to reproduce the representations of metrical values of his copy, that he introduced his own variants of elisions for those of his copy, and made other 'improvements' to the text which affected the metre. In short, these were orthographical matters over which he exercised complete control. A scribe who took such liberties with a Jonsonian manuscript would not flourish, and it is perhaps significant that Herford and Simpson made no alterations which affected the metre in their edition of Pleasure Reconciled to Virtue, for which the copytext was Crane's transcript. Holograph corrections in the Game transcripts show that Middleton was not indifferent to the correctness of the transcripts and Crane may have been impelled to take greater care, at least with the early copies, by the thought that his work was to be overseen by the author. Whether Crane would be scrupulous when the author or an editor was not on hand to check his accuracy, as when the copy for the Folio was prepared, perhaps, is another matter.

The only recent discussion of Crane's accuracy of any length is by J. M. Nosworthy: his conclusions warrant close examination. He writes:

> His transcript of Fletcher's Demetrius and Enanthe, for which the Folio of 1647 serves as a basis of comparison, appears to introduce about sixty errors, of which some twenty relate to stage-directions, into a play consisting of

3,356 typographical lines. For The Witch, comprising 2,187 typographical lines, checking is possible only in respect of the songs quoted and of sporadic paraphrases of Reginald Scot. Even so, the palpable textual errors and suspect readings recorded by Wilson and Greg amount to forty, in addition to which there are five errors in stage-directions. The implication is that Crane's work was variable and never entirely reliable, and the fore-going collations are disturbing since, when all adjustments and allowances have been made, they suggest that he was capable of one error per ten or twelve lines.[57]

This pessimistic view does not seem to be supported by Nosworthy's own figures, for, when the 60 errors of Demetrius and the 45 of The Witch are divided into the total number of typographical lines in these plays, the result is one error in 52 lines, roughly one in each two pages. Divided into the total number of words, the result is an error to every 414 words. But even this does not fairly represent Crane's proneness to error for some of the errors noted by editors should not be laid to his charge. Apart from the places at which the correct reading is uncertain, there are many points at which Crane's copy, and his fidelity to it, brought about the transmission of error.

The collations of some modern editions give an opportunity to categorise the errors in some of his transcripts and to assess his accuracy more exactly. Jonson's Pleasure can be dealt with summarily since Herford and Simpson found that 'its lapses are trivial' and recorded only two substantial errors.[58] They were at 1.94 ('her/are') and 1.244 (Dœdulus/Dædalus'): the

second is probably a misreading for when next the scribe
encountered the word, he spelled it correctly. The <u>Game</u>
transcripts are contaminated by Middleton's revisions,
and comparison of the Trinity and Folger transcripts is
not as useful as might be thought. Nevertheless, collation
of the lines shared by <u>Game</u> Lansdowne and the abbreviated
Malone transcript reveals the extent of Crane's influence
on the readings of the text. My collation takes no
account of stage-directions and elisions, which I have
already discussed. There are 39 errors by comparison with
Middleton's Trinity manuscript, of which 13 are in
Lansdowne and 27 in Malone. (See Appendix 1 for a list
of these variants). There are nine substitutions of words
of small significance (pronouns and prepositions) and
variation of singular or plural nouns and the like. There
are eight other substitutions of greater significance,
generally of words which are broadly synonymous, of which
three more seriously change the meaning of the text. They
are 'publique/privat' at 1.1.289, 'thy/my' at 2.1.137,
and 'our <u>Faithes</u>, or Praires, / our <u>Faithes</u>: our <u>Praiers</u>,'
at 5.3.120. There are two minor additions at 2.1.117
and 4.2.59 where he inserted a pronoun where <u>Game</u>
Lansdowne had only an apostrophe, and 'help: help: oh
help.' for Trinity 'helpe, o helpe' at 2.1.155 and 'well
indeed with' for Trinity 'well with' at 4.4.98. Minor
omissions occur at 2.1.154, 4.2.120, 4.4.17 and 5.3.201.
There are two errors involving speech-prefixes in <u>Game</u>
Malone and one in Lansdowne, at 4.4.87, 5.2.122, and
4.1.126 respectively. In addition <u>Game</u> Malone has four
readings at 2.1.167, 2.2.35, 2.2.96 and 3.1.46-7 which
probably were intended to improve the flow of the shortened
text. They probably should not be regarded as errors

although Crane, if he made the revision, was responsible for them. There are five other more substantial differences between *Game* Lansdowne and Malone which are not supported by the Trinity manuscript. These too were additions made during revision. When allowance is made for revision and obvious mechanical slips (the speech-prefix variants, and 'no[t]' at 1.1.81) and the two expanded apostrophes, there remain twenty-two errors in the 12,427 words (including stage-directions) common to these transcripts. This figure does not seem to support the conclusion that Crane was not reasonably accurate. There are no errors which could be attributed to misreading: Crane could read his own hand.

For collations of the transcripts he made from authorial copy I have used the Malone Society reprints. In *Witch* I find sixteen errors which may be characterised as misreadings: although most of these are common minim errors, some reflect also a deeper misunderstanding of the text, rooted, probably, in the difficult of Middleton's handwriting. (See Appendix 2 for a list of the conjectural emendations in *Witch*). Another group of seven errors may also include misreadings but some variants consist of omitted letters, a kind of error which occurs sporadically but not frequently in his transcripts. There are four speech-prefix errors, in two of which (at l. 1768, 1771) he was probably following copy. Stage-directions are omitted or differ substantially from those in edited texts in twenty-one places: I am reluctant to accept these as evidence of Crane's carelessness for I do not agree with Greg that Crane's copy was the prompt-book. Indeed an entry for 'Sebastian' at l. 1767, and the appropriate (incorrect) speech-prefixes at l. 1768 and 1771 where 'Antonio' is correct may well show that his copy was authorial, since it is unlikely that the promptbook would preserve an error of this kind. Crane's reading 'King's' at l. 46 for 'Duke's' is also probably that of his copy. I find twenty-four clear errors in Crane's transcript. Again, this does not seem to be a large number in light of the probable difficulty (if Game Trinity is representative) of his copy. This is not to say, of course, that they are not important for the text, or that the total takes account of all his mistakes, but there is little support for Nosworthy's view here.

A surer check is given by comparison of Demetrius with The Humourous Lieutenant of the Beaumont and Fletcher Folio of 1647, for which I have used the Malone Society reprint's collation. (See Appendix 3 for a list of these variants). It is reasonable to disregard the sixteen stage-directions which are found only in the Folio text as it was printed from the prompt-book. One variant reading at l. 672 ('sure/Death'), seven readings involving speech-prefixes, ten instances of line rearrangement, and a punctuation variant at l. 914 may also be discounted as ambiguous. This leaves twenty-seven errors, of which eighteen are either the result of misreading or examples of the kind of memorial corruption which occurs when the scribe carries the line in his mind as he writes it out.[59]

An editor receives little aid from knowledge that a scribe made a certain number of errors in so many lines of text if he cannot detect where the errors occur, but he may be encouraged to emend a difficult passage which might

otherwise have been left unaltered if he knows that a
scribe was frequently careless or high-handed. He is more
greatly assisted by knowing what kinds of errors were
likely to be in the text. I do not notice anything distinctive about the errors in Crane's transcripts which
would enable an editor to emend passages where his
critical acuity had not already suspected corruption.
Substitution of epithets, variation of person and tense,
minim errors and misreadings of letters often mistaken
in secretary hand are common kinds of errors which are not
peculiar to Crane. Errors such as 'no' for 'not', or
'thou' for 'though', where the scribe has passed too
quickly to the next word of the text are doubtfully more
characteristic, but in a printed text they can hardly be
distinguished from compositorial misprints. The number
of errors affecting the sense of the text in Crane's
transcripts is relatively small, but nevertheless, his
influence on the text was important. His freeness in
transcribing stage-directions, in normalising speech-
prefixes, and in substituting different elisions for
those of his copy, his great influence on punctuation
and other orthographical matters such as word-compounds,
together with the substantive errors he made, seriously
affect the authority of texts printed from his transcripts.
It cannot be believed that transcription by Crane affected
only superficial, accidental features of the text, for in
many particulars the meaning and emphasis of what the
author had written has been changed, and the cumulative
effect of his orthographical alterations is great.
Mr. Nosworthy is surely correct when he refers to 'the
strong probability that numerous trivial and unveri-
fiable errors were transferred from Crane to the Folio'.[60]

SCRIBAL PRACTICES IN TRANSCRIPTS   61

and it is more than likely that many instances of the
kinds of errors which have been identified by collating
his transcripts with collateral texts will remain
undetected even though an editor may thoroughly understand Crane's habits and the way in which he influenced
the text of his transcripts.

SPELLING

The main orthographical characteristic of a Crane
transcript, obviously, is his spelling. Knowledge of his
spelling habits is important for these reasons. If the
occasional spellings of the Folio texts in which his
influence has been suspected are not consistent with what
is known of his habits, it will be reasonable to doubt
whether they were printed directly from his transcripts.
Further, once the main question has been resolved, knowledge of the spellings of the copy from which the Folio
compositors set their texts may throw some light on the
leading cruxes in these texts. Space does not allow me
to present all the information I have about Crane
spelling habits, so the general characteristics of his
spellings will be summarised and discussion of particular
points which may be relevant to individual texts will be
reserved to later chapters.

From the first examination of the spelling of
Crane's transcripts a list of some 2,200 preferred
spellings from a sample of about 92,000 words was compiled.[61] This included his dedications and holographic
Summary, and the various poetical manuscripts which he
transcribed between 1626 and 1632. As only relatively

small samples of some of the dramatic transcripts which are most pertinent to the present investigation were used, the list was not as full as it could have been made. My object was to identify strong or preferred spellings in different transcripts, but when a spelling variant occurred in many transcripts it was added to the list on the ground that Crane had shown his preference for the spelling on a number of separate occasions, often against the spelling of his copy. These spellings were not only alternative spellings of words for which he had already indicated a preference numerically but also spellings which, although they had not occurred often enough in particular transcripts for it to be clear that they were his and not copy-spellings, occurred many times from transcript to transcript made from copy written by different authors. To this list were added provisionally from the dedications 374 spellings which had not been used often enough for him to have had opportunity to indicate a preference. The presumption is that these were his normal spellings, as he had not been influenced by copy. Finally, about 1,200 'reconstructed' spellings were added. These were spellings which were morphologically-consistent with spellings already on the list. It seems reasonable that if he consistently preferred '-er' for comparatives, to take a simple example, it is safe to infer comparatives spelled in this way for other words on the list, so long as these 'reconstructed' spellings were not incompatible with other spellings in the transcripts. The intention of adding such 'reconstructed' or inferential spellings was to obtain as extensive a list as possible in order to diminish the discrepancy between the vocabularies of the transcripts and the Folio texts which are to be examined.

The morphological reconstructions were limited to a few simple kinds: (a) construction of plurals when the singular ended in '-e' by the addition of '-s', but not the construction of singular nouns of plurals ending with '-es' as the terminal '-e' was sometimes dropped; (b) construction of plural nouns after consonants by the addition of '-s'; (c) the addition of '-r' or '-er' to form nouns of instrument, e.g. 'bearer', or comparatives; (d) the addition of '-st' or '-est' to form superlatives; (e) the addition of '-ing' after consonants, unless there was a possibility that a doubled consonant might have been dropped, and after verbs which ended with '-e', where the terminal '-e' was dropped, as in 'blame/blaming'; and (f) the addition of '-ly' to form adverbs.

The list of preferred, dedication and 'reconstructed' spellings which resulted from this process was tested in two ways. The list was sorted into alphabetical order from the last letter of the spelling so that any inconsistent terminations could be detected and removed. All spellings remaining were then checked against the spellings of the dramatic transcripts so that reconstructions which were contrary to spellings in the transcripts could be removed: when this was done, all the 'reconstructed' spellings were found to be valid. Some 390 spellings in the dramatic transcripts which were morphologically related to words on the list were incorporated: these were infrequent spellings which were consistent with spellings in the transcripts. The list of Crane's spellings now consisted of about 4,200 words comprising the following categories: (1) spellings preferred in the transcripts; (2) spellings preferred in Crane's dedications; (3) other dedication spellings which were morphologically consistent with the spellings of groups (1) and (2); (4) spellings which were morphologically related to his preferred spellings: many of these occurred as alternative spellings in the transcripts.

The main general characteristics of Crane's spelling can be summarised briefly. Exceptions may be found in his transcripts, but the infrequency of such spellings and the conditions under which they occur usually reveal them to be 'copy' spellings. The spellings on this list reveal several morphological invariants:

-ei-	never	-ie-	hence,	feirce
-lly	"	-ly		principally
-ing	"	-eing		shining
-nck	"	-nk		thinck
-ll	"	-l		beutifull
-ncks	"	-nckes		thincks

-s for plurals of nouns with short vowels, never -es,
                                        hence, bands, robbs
-es for plurals of nouns ending in -th/sh/ch, never -s,
                                        hence, clothes,
                                        dishes, riches
-ings for words ending in -ing, never -inges,
                                        hence, tidings
-s or -sse- never -ss, consequently -fes (profes),
    -les (godles), -nes (sadnes), and -asse (passe),
    -esse (progresse), -isse (kisse), -osse (crosse),
    -rsse (worsse)

SCRIBAL PRACTICES IN TRANSCRIPTS 65

The following consonants are never found doubled terminally: g,h,j,k,m,n,p,s,w,x,z. These consonants after long vowels are always found with terminal -e: c,d,f,g, k,l,m,n,p,r,s,v. The following consonants after short vowels are always found with terminal -e: c (sence), voiced g (pledge, spunge), l (resemble), v (twelve) but never after a short vowel and d,f, unvoiced g,h,k,m,n,p and t. Consonants are generally doubled after short vowels in medial positions:

b: not before 'd/ed, e.g., rob'd; b is doubled before
    -ing after short vowels.
d: not doubled before -s, -es, -ing, -er.
g: not doubled before -ing, -er, -es, but probably
    doubled after a short vowel when
    not voiced, e.g., rag/raggs.
l: doubled consonants are retained before -ed but often
    one -l is dropped before -'d, e.g.,
    kil'd, fulfil'd, cal'd/call'd,
    pull'd; after short vowels, e.g.,
    challenge, pallaces, mallice; and
    before -ing and -nes. The consonant is single before -es, but
    funeralls/funerals, ghospells/
    ghospels show that occasionally it
    is also single before -s.
m: doubled medially only after short vowels, e.g., comming,
    but not before -es or -s, e.g., rams.
n: doubled medially after short vowels, e.g., cannon,
    sinners, son/sonnes, but not after
    long vowels or before -s, e.g., sins,
    runs.
p: generally not doubled medially, but note bishopps, lipps.

r:. doubled after short vowels, e.g., horrid, carry, burry.
s: doubled after short vowels.
t: doubled after short vowels and before -ing, e.g., setting, sitting, and -s, but single before -ie (except for cittie and pittie) and -le, e.g., gentle, little, and -es.
w: always single.
z: always single.

Also worthy to notice is Crane's preference for '-w-' in such spellings as plowgh'd, hewgher, lowd, prowd, fowre, rowse, for internal '-a-' in spellings like doated, stroake, yoake, theame, groane, compleate, coales, raak'd, seaven and roabes, and for '-que' in spellings like politique and heroique. Internal '-y-' occurs in such spellings as busynes, byn, grym, nyce, ruyn, rayne, poyson, fayne and wayt, but no clear pattern emerges. His use of '-a-/-au-' shows that he was indifferent to the spelling of acceptance/acceptaunce, acquaintance/acquaintaunce and the like.

Before I leave Crane's spellings, it is interesting to observe his practice with words which have been used to identify the stints of Jaggard's compositors in the Folio. The strongly-preferred spellings are in italics:

ancient 3   Two of these occur in Fletcher texts.
auncient 11
ben 5
bin 1   No '-ee-' spelling occurs.
byn 108
blood 89   No other spelling occurs.

SCRIBAL PRACTICES IN TRANSCRIPTS 67

deare 3
deere 53

deuil/l 85
diuel/l 2

do 35   Fletcher's Barnavelt and Demetrius
doe 345   account for 27 of the 'do' spellings,
doo 2   Pleasure for 4. 'Doo' is in Jonson's
                       Pleasure.

n/either 51   No other spelling occurs.

goe 130   No other spelling occurs.

greefe 1   'Greefe' in Game Folger, 'grief/ue'
greif/ue 41   in Barnavelt, Witch and Demetrius.
grief/ue 3

guift 12   No other spelling occurs.

heire 10   No other spelling occurs.

here 229   In addition there are 48 'here's'
heere 9   and 24 'heer's' spellings.

houre 1
howre 61

ile 39   Pleasure 2; Barnavelt 37.
I'll 247

indeed 46   No other spelling occurs.

mistris 22   'Mistresse' and 'mistrisse' are in
mistresse 3   Demetrius.
mistrisse 1

note 27   No other spelling occurs.

o 67   Fletcher's Barnavelt and Demetrius
oh 179   account for 58 'o's.

raigne 6   No other spelling occurs.

shew 11
show 71

sirha 19   No other spelling occurs.

sodaine 45
suddeine 1

traitor 17
traytor 2

vertue 155
virtue 1

yeare 30		The distribution of these spellings
yeere 43		suggests that Crane had no firm preference.

<u>yong</u> 47
yong 1

    Although Crane's preferences are clear from these figures, the counts for two spellings are not favourable for the examination of the Folio texts. The relatively large number of 'do' spellings suggests that Crane might have been inclined to accept a fair number of these from his copy. Further, the figures for 'ile' make it hard to decide what his preferred spelling was at the time when he was likely to have been preparing copy for the Folio. It is difficult to imagine that he altered his spelling from 'ile' in 1619 to 'I'll' in 1624 without mixing the spellings, but it is possible that any Folio copy he transcribed could have shown either spelling. The more likely spelling cannot be decided.

4. CRANE'S INFLUENCE IN THE FIVE COMEDIES

The examination of Crane's scribal habits in his dramatic transcripts and what is known of the practices of the Folio compositors in the comedies goes far to supply the information necessary to decide the question of his influence in some of the Folio comedies. There are, nevertheless, many matters on which certainty is not likely to be reached. Greg concluded that Tmp., MM and WT were printed from Crane's transcripts of foul papers; TGV and Wiv., he thought, were transcribed from prompt copy. If his view is correct, the scribe's task in preparing printer's copy was conceivably easier for TGV and Wiv. than for the other texts. Although it is possible to believe that he might have been less constrained by copy when transcribing relatively clean prompt copy, it is difficult to decide how foul papers might have affected him, especially as foul papers would probably have been uneven in character. If his attention had been engaged by the author's inconsistencies, and by obscurities in copy, he might not have paid much attention in his transcripts from foul papers to mere orthography and calligraphic ornament. In any event, it is unwise to assume that the orthographical and accidental characteristics of any transcripts Crane made for the Folio were consistent and uniform from one transcript to the other. It is important to know what kind of copy he transcribed, but unfortunately, as Greg's discussion shows,[62] Crane's influence on those features of the text which usually supply good evidence of the character of the underlying text makes it difficult to decide what his copy was in texts printed from his transcripts.[63]

The quality of Crane's transcripts must also have been influenced by the order in which they were made. Hinman's account of the printing of the Folio reveals no delay in printing which can be attributed to unavailability of copy to Jaggard's compositors before the printing of TN. The first plays, where Crane's influence has been suspected, must have been in the printing house before the beginning of 1622.[64] Probably, if Crane made transcripts for the Folio, they were made some time earlier, though in what order, it is not possible at the moment to determine.[65] Of course, if the transcripts were originally intended for another use, they could have been made much earlier, possibly even before the transcript of Barnavelt in 1619, although there is no evidence of this. Hinman concludes that WT was not available to be printed before December, 1622, so if a transcript was prepared by Crane, it must have been made after any other transcripts he made for the Folio.[66] Therefore, the scribe's habits would have been influenced both by the character of the copy before him, and by his increasing familiarity with the kind of material he had to work from. It can be guessed that he did not set out to prepare copy for the printer differently from transcripts made for authors or patrons but it is reasonable to suspect that he would not have been inclined to give the appearance of copy intended for the printer much attention. However, for all that is known, the copy may have been intended to be returned to the King's men for other use and that therefore Crane did attend to the calligraphy of these transcripts.[67] But it is best not to pursue discussion of such possibilities since only the printed texts, if Crane transcribed copy for them, provide real evidence of his methods.

Another influence on the characteristics of possible Crane copy for the Folio is the language of the text he had for transcription. An author like Middleton whose style was naturally elliptical gave many opportunities for Crane to indicate elision, syncopation and other orthographical refinements, but the language of the early TGV does not afford the opportunity for sophistication given by the late plays, Tmp. and WT. The extent to which the author used vocatives, more frequent in Wiv. than in the other plays, would also affect a scribe's tendency to supply parentheses. It is not surprising then, that the orthographical and textual peculiarities that have led to the association of Crane with some Folio comedies are most frequent in the last mentioned plays.

The textual characteristics adduced to show that Crane influenced the texts of the early comedies are mainly accidentals --- marks of elision, parentheses, hyphens and the like --- and matters of substance supply little evidence for identification of the texts for which he made transcripts.[68] His control over the accidentals of copy he transcribed was so strong, and his regard for the forms of his copy so small, that little is likely to be learned about the accidentals of his copy from texts printed from his transcripts. However, the relative consistency of accidentals does give good evidence for detecting his influence in the Folio. Nevertheless, since he consciously altered his text most greatly in transcripts he made from copy in his own hand, his influence on substantives is not likely to have been as great in the Folio as it was in <u>Game</u> Malone. There will, however, be errors of transcription: these, by their nature, will be difficult to distinguish from compositorial errors.

The general character of a Crane transcript for the Folio is readily deduced from what has been seen of his habits in his other dramatic transcripts. His transcripts probably contained clear and correct act and scene markings, and in some of them the entrances might be massed at the beginning of each scene, with consequent though not complete loss of later entrances and most other stage-directions. His stage-directions had features which might be characterised as 'literary' and attributed to his copy, but his interference with the text of stage-directions makes them doubtful evidence for the kind of copy he transcribed. Orthographical distinctions would be well and probably consistently marked, but there might well have been some inconsistency in representing elisions. Conventional elisions might have been expanded into the 'Jonsonian' form, whereas Jonsonian elisions in his copy might have lost the apostrophes indicating the elision, to the detriment of the metre. Crane's often slapdash writing of apostrophes could have led the compositors to overlook them in such elisions. The handwriting of the transcript would have been clear, and liberal italicisation would have distinguished headings, directions, proper nouns and other words requiring emphasis from the dialogue. Punctuation would be heavy, with numerous colons, hyphens, and parentheses. Apart from the overall sophistication, the transcript would have represented the author's text with considerable accuracy, but the scribe's interference with stage-directions and metre would have compromised the authority of the text for modern readers.

It is less easy to deduce to what extent these features would have occurred in a particular transcript made for the Folio. The preparation of Barnavelt was nearer the start of printing of the Folio than Crane's other dramatic transcripts, and it might be thought that Folio copy would resemble that transcript in many of its characteristics. But Barnavelt was made to be used as a prompt-book and it is not typical of Crane's usual transcripts. It is not as calligraphic or as heavily punctuated as, say, Game Folger, which, in view of the special character of Barnavelt, Folio copy is most likely to have resembled, if a single model is to be selected. At question here is what kinds of embellishment Crane supplied to any Folio copy (massed entrances are not found in all the texts he has been associated with, for example) and how frequent or strong such features as punctuation and hyphenation were in any particular transcript. Because no Crane transcript survives between the 1619 Barnavelt and the 1624 Game, there is no direct evidence of his habits during the period which is most interesting. Accordingly, the absence of a particular characteristic of Crane's from a particular text need not necessarily tell against his influence on the preparation of copy for the Folio.

Care must be taken, furthermore, to distinguish evidence which might simply be due to compositorial normalisation, and evidence which can be used to show that a particular characteristic was taken over from the copy from which the text has been printed. In short, some kinds of evidence of Crane's influence may be impossible to find in one text or the other simply because it was not characteristic of the way in which he prepared the particular transcript. Other kinds of evidence may be undetectable because the compositors normalised features of their copy according to their general practice. It is not to be expected that many peculiarities of the accidentals of copy will survive compositorial attention. Sometimes a compositor may unthinkingly reproduce more or less exactly what he saw before him, and sometimes he might allow his copy to prevail in a matter such as distinction of names in stage-directions when he had no preference or precedent. In general, however, conformity and uniformity are the rule in the Folio rather than diversity and individuality in typographical matters. Hence arises much of the difficulty of compositor identifications and the relatively great weight that is put on departures from normal or preferred practices. I am disposed therefore to attach some importance to the compositors' reproduction of accidentals which can be identified as Crane's.

ACCIDENTALS

I propose firstly to discuss the accidentals of the five comedies in relation to what is known or what can be deduced about normal typographical practice in the Folio, and then to pass on to the evidence of massed stage-directions, parentheses, hyphenation, elisions and the like which have been accepted as evidence of Crane's influence by F. P. Wilson, Greg, Dover Wilson and the New Arden editors. This general view of the kinds of evidence should allow each play to be discussed in turn and the particular implications of Crane's transcription to be examined in more detail.

The earliest sign of Crane's influence in the Folio comedies occurs on A1 of <u>Tmp</u>., which was set by compositor B: it was the first page of the Folio to be set into type. There alone is a scene heading in roman rather than italic type.[69] If <u>Tmp</u>. had been set from a Crane transcript this might readily be explained by the influence of his bold hand in act and scene headings on a compositor who had not yet settled on a suitable way of representing the headings in type. On the other hand, this might simply arise from experimentation with no reference at all to copy; by itself 'Scena Secunda' has little value as evidence.

Another characteristic of the typography of the early comedies may have been influenced by Crane's practice of distinguishing the names of characters in stage-directions by writing them in his bold italic hand.[70] Most of the Folio stage-directions were set entirely in italic but I have noticed thirty-eight in which roman and italic type is mixed. Most of these have only the personal nouns in roman but in Err. at l. 1103, compositor B set 'Enter Adriana and Luciana', and compositor A(F) started TGV in the same style with the first entrance, 'Valentine: Protheus, and Speed'. At l. 62 of MV, compositor C changed the italic of his quarto copy to set 'Enter Bassanio, Lorenso, and Gratiano'. In TGV, since the direction lacks the preliminary 'Enter', an omission in accord with Crane's practice in massed entrances, it is quite likely that 'and' was in Crane's secretary hand, but the other instances are more likely to reflect compositorial inadvertance. Occasionally there are other words in roman in italic stage-directions or other passages of text in italic, but when these were not compositorial errors they illustrate the converse distinction exemplified by A's '... Southwell reades, Coniuro te, &c ...' at 2H6 644. Sometimes too, text which was normally italicised was printed in roman in order to distinguish it from a preceding passage in italic type.[71]

There are insufficient instances of italic/roman distinction to allow compositorial habits to be deduced, and they are so few that, where the compositor was not manifestly careless, the influence of copy can be suspected. The twelve instances of this in texts set from quarto copy show that when the compositors did not follow the distinctions of their copy, or did not observe their usual practice in the Folio, they maintained the distinctions of their copy by setting roman for italic and italic for roman. Little can be learned from these texts and, without copy, other occurrences in other texts printed from manuscript copy are also not helpful.

However, in Tmp., TGV and Wiv., that is, the first three texts to be set up, the fifteen passages, some of them stage-directions, containing names in roman type (a greater number than in all the other texts together) suggest that the compositors had been influenced by a feature of their copy.[72] All but three instances, set by compositor A(F), are on C's pages, but as he was not prone to make this distinction elsewhere in the Folio, they cannot be attributed solely to him. Although C set much of MM, none of the stage-directions there has names in roman type. In WT there are two longer passages in which roman names are conspicuous, the indictment of Hermione at l. 1187-95 and the response of the Delphic oracle at l. 1313-16, both set by compositor A. The typography is just what might be expected if the compositor had had Crane's calligraphic transcript before him.

In TGV compositor C set one of the 'names of the actors' in italic: it is possible that if the copy of TGV was in Crane's hand, the list of characters in the play had also been written by him. The tables of characters at the end of 2H4 and Tim. were printed, according to Hinman, merely to fill space, as too, perhaps, was that for Oth.[73] There are eight such lists in the Folio. Greg considered that only the list at the end of Tmp. was certainly printed because it was in the copy and not specially supplied to fill space.[74] However, it is hardly conceivable that a compositor would have held up work on the Folio to allow space-filling lists to be compiled if they were not already part of the copy, and

the order of printing gives no support for the view that
this happened. Whatever the reason they were printed,
they were already available in the compositors' copy:
when they were not, the compositors did not hesitate to
leave a blank page if the sequence of printing made it
necessary. The character of the lists and the provision
of the name of the duke in MM makes it highly improbable
that the compositors compiled them themselves as necessary.
Therefore it is probably significant that four of the
five plays with which Crane has been associated supply
lists of actors. (There was insufficient space on the
page for a list to be printed for Wiv.) Similar lists
for Witch and quarto Duchess of Malfi, which was
printed from a Crane transcript, suggest that it was his
practice to supply his transcripts with lists of
characters, though whether he compiled them himself or
copied them cannot be determined.

Little can be gathered from the compositors' arrangement of stage-directions in which, it may be assumed, they
followed whatever practice was typographically convenient.
Some of the longer descriptive stage-directions for stage
business, like those at l. 1535-8 and 1616-18 of Tmp. are
indented in a manner consistent with Crane's practice in
his transcripts, but the variation of this arrangement
from page to page confirms the probability that it owed
more to the compositors than to copy. Of the twenty-
five stage-directions longer than one line of type in C's
pages, twenty-one are of this kind, that is, the first
line extends to the width of the column and successive
lines are indented from two to four characters' width
beneath.[75]

An important characteristic of the stage-directions in the five comedies is the massed entrances which are found in TGV, Wiv. and WT but not in Tmp. and MM. In the last directions for action within scenes are infrequent, as they are in Wiv., but the directions of Tmp. are extensive and descriptive: their character is similar to that of Crane's Game transcripts. Particular peculiarities may best be considered in the following chapter, but notice should be taken here of Crane's use of massed entrances without the usual preliminary 'Enter'. This is lacking in TGV in directions on B4^V and C6^V and in Wiv. on E1, the first two pages set by F (as I designate the 'A' compositor before WT) and the other by compositor B. The massed entrances of Duchess of Malfi also have no preliminary 'Enter'.

It is not necessary to give credence to Dover Wilson's view that texts with massed entrances had been assembled from the plot and actors' parts and Crane's use of such directions should be accounted for in some other way. This is not easy. It is scarcely to be believed that he thought that these directions would make the comedies easier to read but he must have imagined that some advantage would accrue, since it must have been more laborious for him to have reconstructed the directions after this pattern than to have transcribed what he had before him in his manuscript copy. It may have been of course that his copy was so deficient that he had no alternative, but this is not likely to have been true of his copy for WT at least. It might be suggested that the scribe noticed that his copy showed the kind of variation of characters' names found in Rom. Q2 for Capulet's wife.

If this offended his natural inclination to tidiness so that he wished to achieve a uniform nomenclature in stage-directions and speech-prefixes, it can be imagined that he listed the characters appearing in each scene at the beginning of it and collated the results when he had finished. He could also have used this for the lists of characters in the play, although, if he did, he did not do it thoroughly.[76] However, this does not explain why he preferred these listing directions to those of his copy and why he omitted directions describing action within scenes and more elaborate descriptive directions, if they were present in his copy. Even the shortened Game Malone has eight marginal and descriptive directions. Also, it is necessary to assume that his copy showed the kind of varied nomenclature which made such a process expedient, but there was no such ambiguity in the characters' names in Game Malone. His use of massed entries for WT is even less understandable, for if, as I have suggested, Crane prepared the new prompt-book before transcribing copy for the printer, there is no conceivable reason other than his choice to follow the model of Jonson's Folio. Nevertheless, the presence of them in three of the five comedies is suggestive evidence of his influence on the copy since the only other texts of this period with similar directions seem also to have come from his pen.[77]

No use can be made of the occurrence of contracted names in stage-directions to demonstrate his influence in the Folio, for although it was sometimes his practice to abbreviate the names of characters, their expansion by compositors obscures the evidence. Contraction in stage-

INFLUENCE IN FIVE COMEDIES   81

directions in <u>Wiv</u>. from page El onwards coincides with
compositor B's share in this text and reveals little of
the forms of the copy. Speech-prefixes too supply little
useful evidence as Crane's speech-prefixes were consistent and there was nothing so unusual about his
practice to enable his speech-prefixes to be distinguished
from the forms favoured by the compositors. The compositors have also obscured anything useful to be observed
from the appearance of italicised words in the dialogue:
there seems to be nothing remarkable about the use of
italics in the five comedies which can be explained by
Crane's influence.

PUNCTUATION MARKS

Other aspects of the texts can be conveniently
examined with the aid of a table of punctuation in ten
Folio comedies. To facilitate consideration of the
punctuation in the five early comedies, the table supplies
figures for five other texts, printed from different kinds
of copy; the texts comprise roughly the same total number
of words as the early comedies. A note of the shares of
the respective compositors is given also. Inspection of
the counts shows, however, that variation of the proportions of a mark of punctuation in different texts cannot
be explained entirely by compositorial influence, although
undoubtedly individual compositors had somewhat different
habits of punctuation and capitalisation.[78]

The relative density of punctuation (which includes
capitalisation) in the groups of texts is given by
dividing the number of words in each text by the total

MARKS OF PUNCTUATION IN TEN FOLIO COMEDIES

PUNCTUAT.	Tmp.	TGV	Wiv.	MM	WT	TOTAL	Err.	Ado.	LLL	Shr.	AWW	TOTAL
Full stop	738	843	926	971	969	4447	645	875	1298	981	1056	4855
Interrog.	197	293	392	347	317	1546	209	274	290	275	214	1262
Exclam.	4	0	0	0	0	4	2	32	6	0	2	42
Colon	615	525	956	659	839	3594	299	321	452	470	459	2001
Semicolon	142	174	175	168	174	833	65	8	55	31	53	212
Commas	1704	1713	2094	2136	2600	10247	1476	2353	2121	2316	2222	10488
Dash	1	3	11	0	5	20	0	0	0	3	7	10
Parenths.	102	139	226	78	371	916	20	26	49	23	15	133
Apostr.	580	391	450	516	994	2931	273	247	252	409	541	1722
Hyphens	143	125	361	93	264	986	47	73	120	71	61	372
Quotat.	0	0	2	1	0	3	0	0	0	0	0	0
Capitals	1152	875	1471	1164	2281	6943	626	753	1128	1127	1014	4648
WORDS	17295	18044	22300	22595	25652	105886	15365	22079	22355	21831	23950	105580
Total punc.	5378	5081	7064	6133	8814	32470	3662	4962	5771	5706	5644	25745

PROPORTION OF PUNCTUATION TO NUMBER OF WORDS IN TEXT

PUNCTUAT.	Tmp.	TGV	Wiv.	MM	WT	AVERAGE	Err.	Ado.	LLL	Shr.	AWW	AVERAGE
Full stop	23	21	24	23	26	24	24	26	17	23	23	23
Interrog.	88	60	57	66	81	70	74	80	77	80	113	85
Exclam.	4324	-	-	-	-	-	7683	690	3726	-	11975	-
Colon	29	34	23	34	31	30	51	69	50	46	52	54
Semicolon	122	104	127	135	147	127	236	2760	406	704	452	912
Comma	10	11	11	11	10	11	10	9	11	9	11	10
Dash	-	6015	2027	-	5130	-	-	-	-	7277	3421	-
Parenths.	170	130	99	290	69	151	768	849	456	949	1597	923
Apostr.	30	46	50	44	26	39	56	90	89	53	44	67
Hyphens	121	144	62	243	98	134	327	302	186	308	392	303
Quotat.	-	-	-	-	-	-	-	-	-	-	-	-
Capitals	15	21	15	19	12	16	25	29	20	19	24	23
Wds/punc.	3.2	3.5	3.1	3.7	3.0	3.3	4.2	4.5	3.9	3.8	4.3	4.1
Comp. F/A	6	9	4	2½	16	37½	8	2½	6	14	21	51½
Comp. B ⎱ Pages	7	-	10	6½	11	34½	4	14½	11	4	2	35½
Comp. C ⎰	6	10	8	10½	-	34½			6		2	20

number of marks of punctuation. In the five early comedies the most heavily punctuated text is WT, the least, MM, but apart from MM, the frequency of punctuation is quite consistent in the texts of this group. Further, all the five early comedies are more densely punctuated than any of the later comedies, which also show a fair measure of consistency. The different densities of punctuation in the two groups suggest that the copy for the five comedies was more heavily punctuated than the copy from which the Folio compositors set the later comedies, and the consistency of the figures for the five comedies further suggests that their copy came from a single source.[79]

There are several particular points of interest in the table, especially when comparison is made with the table of punctuation in Crane's dramatic transcripts.[80] The figures for Crane's earliest transcripts, Pleasure (1618) and Barnavelt (1619), of the proportion of punctuation to words, 3·6 and 3·9 respectively, are close to the proportion of punctuation to words of MM which is about the same length as Barnavelt. Comparison of the overall proportions of the transcripts and the five comedies shows them to be consistent with Crane's preparation of copy for the Folio before 1622 and, if the figures for the comedies are a good guide, and if the copy was his, the general level of punctuation probably approached that of Barnavelt. As Crane's punctuation became heavier over the years and when he transcribed his own transcripts, the figure for WT is consistent with the certainty that its copy was prepared last of all, and possibly with its preparation from an earlier Crane transcript. It is conceivable that the figures for density of punctuation reveal, as WT suggests, the order in which the transcripts were prepared, if they came from the same pen, but a more detailed analysis of the punctuation figures would be necessary to enable the texts to be arranged in order of transcription on this evidence alone. Nevertheless, I have suggested a likely order in the next chapter.[81]

The proportions of capitals to total number of words are also consistent with what has been seen of Crane's habits in his transcripts.[82] The proportions for Tmp. and Wiv. agree with those for Pleasure (15) and Barnavelt (16) whereas capitals in TGV and MM are somewhat less frequent, and in WT, more frequent. The character of the capitalisation in the five comedies, apart from its frequency, is not distinctive as indeed it was not in Crane's transcripts. Again capitals in the second group of comedies are not as frequent generally as they are in the early comedies and although a more rigorous statistical analysis might enable some allowance to be made for different compositorial habits, it would be surprising to find that the different proportions of capitals were solely because of compositorial differences and not also attributable to varying characteristics of the copy from which the later comedies were set. The figures do allow a tentative conclusion that much of the capitalisation in these texts reproduces what the compositors found in their copy, although, if this is correct, editors will not be able to determine whether any particular use of a capital can be attributed to compositor or copy.

Capitals are a useful guide to the characteristics of copy because unlike the proportions of full stops, interrogation and exclamation marks, colons, semicolons, commas, parentheses and dashes, the proportions do not vary in a complex manner on account of the use of different means of pointing, like the use of commas, parentheses, or dashes to mark off parentheses. The proportion of full stops, even though they are affected by the use of other marks of punctuation in a particular text, do not vary greatly amongst the texts of both groups, and this fact, and comparison with the proportions in Crane's transcripts (where they are not nearly as frequent) suggests that the compositors greatly influenced this kind of pointing.[83] Exclamation marks are generally infrequent in the comedies; the greatest number occurs in Ado. where they have been reproduced from quarto copy. It seems also that Jaggard's compositors at least did not trouble themselves to distinguish exclamation from interrogation marks when setting from manuscript copy. TGV, Wiv. and MM share a relatively high proportion of interrogation marks which is not characteristic of Tmp. and WT or the five other comedies.

Colons, which Crane favoured, are relatively frequent in the early comedies by comparison with the later, and the proportions there are comparable to those of his transcripts. Semicolons too are very frequent in the five comedies, but variation of the figures for these texts and by comparison with the counts for the transcripts suggests that the compositors have influenced the frequency of semicolons, and colons, more greatly here than other marks of punctuation. WT has a lower proportion of colons and semicolons than might have been expected, but this is compensated for by the great number of commas. However, the uniform distribution of commas throughout all ten comedies and the observation that there are more in the printed texts than in Crane's dramatic transcripts makes it certain that many of the commas in the comedies were added by the compositors.

Thus far, the punctuation of the five comedies is consistent with that which might be expected from texts set from Crane transcripts, but because the proportions of alternative marks of punctuation vary, and because composition affected the frequency of some kinds of punctuation, it is not possible to conclude from this evidence that the compositors' copy for the five comedies was characterised by Crane's habits of punctuation. Clearer evidence is supplied by the counts of apostrophes and hyphens, often mentioned as characteristic of Crane's influence in the comedies, for their use is not greatly affected by other punctuation. Parentheses, which Greg noticed were used 'lavishly'[84] in the early comedies, may alternate with commas, but the marked difference between their proportions in the two groups strongly suggests that they were frequent in the copy for the early texts. The proportions vary considerably: WT has a number consistent with its later transcription (if the copy was prepared by Crane) or with the copy having been transcribed from an earlier Crane transcript. The overall frequency of parentheses is like that of Crane's early transcripts of Pleasure and Barnavelt, and the low number in MM is very close to the number in Barnavelt. The compositors may have been responsible for many of the parentheses in these texts, particularly parentheses around vocatives which are most frequent in Wiv.[85] Since it has been seen that Crane was not inclined to favour parentheses with vocatives in transcripts from authorial copy[86] it is useful to consider the relative proportions of some words used vocatively with and without parentheses in the five comedies.[87] These figures make no allowance for the compositors' reluctance to use parentheses around a vocative at the beginning of a line and may therefore be of doubtful validity. Only in Wiv. is there a greater number of vocative parentheses than others; of the possible situations where parentheses could have been used, 35% of the vocatives in Wiv. have them. The proportions for the other texts are: Tmp. 11%; TGV 23%; MM 4% and WT 39%. The texts with the greatest proportions of vocatives in parentheses are those with the greatest number of parentheses of all kinds. This, together with the variation amongst the five early comedies and the higher proportions of vocatives with parentheses in Crane's dramatic transcripts, suggests that the compositors tended to reproduce parentheses from copy, or to ignore them, rather than to add them when they were not in their copy. But little can be said about this until more is known of the individual compositors' habits. In the meantime it is sufficient to notice that the disparity in the use of parentheses between the early and later comedies suggests that the copy for the first group had a common origin.

Apostrophes in the two groups of comedies present much the same picture; only in AWW, which Greg thought was printed from foul papers, are they as frequent as they were in any of the five comedies.[88] The proportions of the five comedies are consistent with the view that the copy was prepared by Crane after he had made the prompt-book of <u>Barnavelt</u> in 1619, although it is likely that had the compositors been setting from Crane copy, they would have used apostrophes more often and more consistently to indicate non-syllabic '-ed' and similar contractions than Crane did.

Particular elisions involving the use of apostrophes reveal more of the special character of the copy for the five comedies than the mere proportions, particularly as some uses of the apostrophe are rare in other texts set by the same compositors. There is also the possibility that Crane transmitted some contractions from Shakespeare's manuscripts.[89] I have examined the occurrence of elisions found in the five comedies in some other comedies printed from manuscript copy: <u>Err</u>., <u>AWW</u>, <u>AYL</u>, <u>Shr</u>. and <u>TN</u>. Two sorts of evidence from elisions are significant. There are elisions which are found in the comedies thought to have been set up from Crane transcripts but rare or absent in the later comedies. 'Eu'n' occurs seven times in the early texts as the contraction of 'euen' or 'euening', three times with a 'v' (Crane, like Hand D of <u>STM</u>, very often used 'v' inside a word after the modern practice) and six times in the later comedies, though never with an internal 'v'; 'e'n' and 'e'ne' occur three times in the later comedies but never in the early texts. 'I'ld' or 'Il'd' is found twelve times in the five comedies as might be expected from Crane's spellings in his dramatic transcripts, but 'Ide' or 'I'de' occurs ten times in the other plays. The only occurrences of Crane's alternative spelling 'I'll' are in <u>MM</u> (2538, 2823, 2830)

and __Tmp__. has 'I'am' (64) whereas __Err__. and __AWW__ have 'I'me'.
The only occurrence in these ten comedies of 'neu'r', a
Crane alternative spelling, is in __Wiv__. 'Thou'rt' occurs
eleven times in the early comedies (with 'th'ourt' in
__AWW__) but there are eight 'th'art's in the later plays.[90]
Similarly, 'you're' occurs only in __WT__. There are only
two Jonsonian apostrophes in the ten comedies, 'I'am' in
__Tmp__. and 'I'haue' in __MM__ (1206). These elisions need not
have been frequent in Crane's copy since his use of them
varied, but, if they were, the compositors took little
notice of the apostrophes.[91]

There is also variation in the use of the apostrophe
to denote elision. Since apostrophes are more frequent
in the five comedies it is not surprising that 29 of the
51 'dost's there have the apostrophe whereas only two of
the 23 in the later comedies have it. 'Hap'ly' occurs
four times in __TGV__, only once without the apostrophe, but
ten times thereafter without it. The only five occurrences
of 'hast' with a redundant apostrophe are in pages A5^V,
C5 and G5^V of the five comedies where compositor A(F) seems
to have followed copy. Apostrophes are also often found
in 'ha's' but as there are many of these throughout the
Folio they are more likely to be compositorial variants
than reflections of copy spellings. The only appearances
of "'pre-thee", a variant most suggestive of Crane, are
in __Tmp__. The five comedies also have six instances of
"'saue" with the apostrophe denoting the omission of 'God'
whereas none of the four instances in the later comedies
has the apostrophe. 'Tane' with the apostrophe in
different positions in the word occurs five times in the
five comedies but only once (in __AYL__) in the later

comedies where 'tane' is found sixteen times without the apostrophe, as it occurs in Addition II of STM.

Apostrophes with the possessive singular of proper nouns ending in vowels are not uncommon in the Folio; I have counted over 140 instances. However, 'it's' is unusual. It occurs eight times in the five comedies, only once without the apostrophe (in MM) and does not occur in the later comedies at all. The use of the modern 'it's' for "'tis" in TGV (4) and TN (4) may indicate that both texts had been transcribed before printing; one might expect a more regular distribution had the elision been a compositorial variant. There are also many other instances of the use of apostrophes in the five comedies which are of greater value as evidence that Crane prepared the copy for the five plays but it is better to discuss them in some detail in connection with the texts in which they occur: this is done in the following chapter. All the forms mentioned above are characteristic of Crane's habits in his transcripts and add to the evidence that the copy for the five comedies came from his pen.

Elaborate hyphenation was also a feature of his transcripts and instances of unusual uses of hyphens, and the frequency of hyphenated compounds, have often been suggested as further evidence of his influence on the Folio comedies. It is interesting to observe that none of the hyphenated compounds in the five comedies (or in Crane's transcripts) contains extreme instances of compounding like 'needy-hollow-ey'd-sharpe-looking-wretch' in Err. (1717). Nor are hyphens used in

Shakespeare's portion of Addition II of <u>STM</u>. The scribe and the Folio compositors must therefore have been responsible for most of the hyphens in the five comedies. The greatest number of the hyphenated-compounds are simple adjective-noun compounds which do not reveal Crane's influence with certainty. The compounds which are more characteristic of his habits are relatively few in number; they are mentioned in the next chapter.

    Although the testimony of the orthographical characteristics which have already been discussed goes far to confirm that Crane prepared copy for some of the Folio comedies, it would stand for little in my estimation were it not confirmed by the evidence of spellings. It requires no further demonstration that although compositors spelled some words consistently in the same way, there were other words for which they had no preferred spelling and which they were disposed to vary in spelling or accept from their copy. Accordingly, it would be impossible to believe that Crane influenced the copy for these plays if the spellings which were contrary to known compositorial preferences were also inconsistent with Crane's known spellings. Further, if it is to be believed that he made transcripts for all five texts, then the spellings which may reasonably be supposed to reflect the spellings of the copy must be consistent within the group of five texts. If on the other hand, he had no part in the preparation of copy for any of these plays, then there should be detectable differences amongst the copy-reflecting spellings of the different comedies. Finally, there should be a negative demonstration that the methods by which his spellings are found in some texts do not

also identify spellings as his in texts which it is very
unlikely he influenced. Such texts may be Shr. and Err.,
which were printed from foul papers, or, for a good
reason, TN which was printed from the prompt-book or a
transcript of it. Unless the residual or copy-reflecting
spellings of these texts are unlike the spellings in the
five comedies it cannot be believed either that Crane
influenced those texts or, alternatively, that the test
of his influence was a good one.

SPELLINGS

    The examination of possible Crane spellings in the
Folio is complicated in many ways.[92] The list of Crane's
spellings does not give a spelling to match all the
words of the early comedies. Sometimes his spelling may
be inferred from morphologically-similar spellings for
which his preference was well established, and for a few
unusual words, spellings in the concordance of his
dramatic transcripts may provide clues to his spelling.
But little or nothing is known of the spellings of the
copy which Crane transcribed and therefore spellings
which passed from copy by way of Crane to the Folio cannot
easily be identified.[93] However, the number of such
spellings cannot be large.

    A greater impediment to the investigation of the
spellings of the Folio comedies is the lack of knowledge about the spellings of the four Jaggard compositors who set them into print. However, a recent
study of the habits of compositor B, who shared the composition of all but TGV of the five comedies, affords the

possibility of detecting spellings which B reproduced from copy.[94] Dr. Kable found that compositor B strongly preferred final '-y' after vowels and in many words, also after some consonants. His preference for '-esse' endings was demonstrated by many spellings. He also examined the appearance of words which had been taken as evidence of B's influence by Miss Walker and other investigators in the Pavier quartos and substantially confirmed their findings. A particularly valuable aspect of Kable's work was that he was able to determine B's spelling of particular words.

Kable's most significant conclusion was that there were words for which B had no preferred spelling and that therefore spellings of them in pages set up by B would probably be the spellings of the copy. The likelihood of this has long been appreciated, but Kable was able to identify over a hundred words for which B was prone to reproduce the spellings of copy and further, to provide an estimate of the probability that a spelling of such a word had been taken from copy.[95] When spellings of 'art, brier, marvel, palace' and 'oh' are found in pages set by B, they are almost certainly the spellings of the copy. Unfortunately, most of B's copy-reflecting spellings are not words which were subject to much variation of spelling in this period, and when allowance has been made for compositorial inconsistency and the effect of justification, Kable's spellings (a large number of which are 'ie/y' variants) are not as helpful as could have been wished. However, I incorporated most of the spellings which Kable mentioned in a list of words which has been used to detect possible copy spellings in the comedies. When a variant spelling of a word on this list occurs, it is, by implication, a spelling which B has reproduced from copy.[96]

Some 149 spellings of the words on this list may be found in the concordance to TN, which was wholly set up by compositor B. Sixteen of these may have arisen from the compositor's need to justify long lines by adding or omitting characters in words; these must be excluded from the evidence although, of course, some of them may be the spellings of the copy. For another 85 words there were no alternative spellings. The remaining spellings should represent the spellings of B's copy and, if Crane had prepared the copy for TN, they would be found on his list of preferred spellings. Kable's B spellings, other spellings in TN, and Crane's preferred spellings of these words may be consulted in a table printed as Appendix 4.

Nineteen of the alternative spellings occur on the Crane spelling list. This may seem to be a high number for a text in which he probably had no part, but the character of the variants shows that there is no ground for surprise. Many of the spellings are binary, that is, there are effectively only two possible spellings of a word like 'act', and it is not remarkable that a fair number of any list of spellings will be found on the Crane spelling list.[97] Twenty-eight variant spellings are not on the Crane list. More significant spellings are those where Crane's spelling was the same as B's: the variation can be explained only by B's inconsistency or, as seems more likely, by copy not written by Crane. If B's copy was in Crane's hand, he departed from their

preferred spellings to set 'ayde, bloudie, bloudy,
cleare, companie, denie, earely, ladie, madde, marrie,
maisters, prettie, readie, verie', and 'willinglie'.
'Young' is one of the spellings for which B was greatly
influenced by copy; this spelling occurs only once in
Crane's dramatic transcripts, yet it occurs in TN. The
most significant variants are those for which Crane's
and B's spellings were different and a third spelling
occurs in TN: instances in the table are 'beauty, breefe,
cosin, country, credit'(which B seems to have used
occasionally), 'together' and 'wee'l'. The test of B's
copy-reflecting spellings shows adequately that Crane did
not prepare the copy for TN.

There are 93 of Kable's compositor B spellings or
variants of them in B's eight pages of Err. (See Appendix
5 for these spellings). Of these 54 must be set aside as
no alternative spellings occur, and there are another four
variants which are likely to have been affected by justification. Seventeen words of the remaining 35 are
represented by variant spellings only: compositor B did
not use his habitual spelling of these words. Most of
the non-B spellings in Err. show variation between '-ie'
and '-y' endings and the number of other spellings which
end in '-ie' suggest that this was a strong characteristic
of the copy. There is no information available about
Crane's spelling of 'aboard' and 'natiuity', and so the
number of B spellings represented by variants is reduced
to 33. Nine of these are found on the Crane spelling
list, but this, as I have remarked before, is not significant. For seventeen of the 24 words for which Crane's
spelling differs from the non-B variant in the Folio text,

if B had been setting from copy in Crane's hand, he would
have been using variant spellings inconsistent with his
preferences in Err. and in other texts. Therefore, it is
reasonable to conclude that the copy for Err. had not been
influenced by Crane.

Compositor B set most of Shr., ten pages, in which
there are 69 copy-reflecting spellings or variants of the
words listed by Kable. (See Appendix 6 for these spellings).
Most of these again are '-ie/y' spellings which must have
been strong in copy for often B did not use his '-y'
spelling at all for such words. The copy may also have
contained mixed 'courtesie/curtesie, loud, oh' spellings,
and 'sodaine' and 'yong', which B was prone to reproduce
from copy. Eleven words which may have been affected by
justification, and another ('dowry') for which there is
no evidence of Crane's spelling, must be set aside. There
remain 57 variant spellings of which 26 occur on the
Crane spelling list. This, as the table shows, is not
significant. What is important here is that there are
29 variants which B set against his usual practice and
against the spelling of his copy if it was in Crane's
hand.[98] Clearly the copy for Shr. had not been prepared
by Crane.

There is considerable evidence of his influence on
WT however, of which B set eleven pages. The same test
can be applied to discover whether B's copy-reflecting
spellings are consistent with the spellings on the Crane
spelling list. Here the table shows that there are 45
variants or copy-reflecting spellings of B's preferred
forms, of which eleven must be set aside as showing the

INFLUENCE IN FIVE COMEDIES 97

effect of justification. No information about Crane's spelling is available for two other words. Other spellings, 'credit, deare, furie' and 'runne' are probably B's alternative or inconsistent spellings, but even if they are not, all the remaining 28 non-B spellings are Crane's. Possibly significant (although these spellings also occur in Shr.) are 'loud, oh' and 'yong' for which B almost invariably reproduced the spelling of his copy. 'Loud/lowd' and 'o/oh' show Crane's habitual mixture of these spellings whereas 'yong' was his invariable spelling. This is good evidence that B's pages in WT were set from Crane copy.

This result encourages inspection by the same method of the other texts in which B shared. In the seven pages of Tmp. set by B there are 31 variants of his usual spelling. Nine of these may have been affected by justification. Eleven of the remaining 22 occur on the Crane spelling list and seven of the others show variation of '-ie/y' which might reflect B's inconsistency.[99] There is no information about Crane's spelling of 'aboard' and 'credit' seems to be B's regular alternative spelling; Crane preferred 'creadit'. 'Pity' for B's 'pitty' and Crane's 'pittie/pitty' might be B's economical spelling, and 'noyse/s' for B's 'noise' might show the influence of Crane's habitual 'noyce' spelling. The variants consistent with Crane's habits show only two spellings of much weight as evidence, 'lowder' and 'pre-thee'. It can scarcely be claimed that this is good evidence that Tmp. was set from a Crane transcript, although the spellings do not show that the copy could not have been Crane's.

Compositor B set ten pages of Wiv. in which some 47 of his habitual or copy-reflecting spellings are represented by variants. Twenty spellings probably show the influence of justification. Nineteen of the remaining spellings are found on the Crane spelling list, and 'deuill, girle, hart, hartlings, iest/s, o/oh, they'll, wee'll' and 'yeere/s' are good testimony of Crane's influence. Eight variants remain: 'she'll' and 'we'll' are probably also Crane spellings as sometimes he did not double the 'e' in such elisions. 'Bloud/y' which occurs also in MM tells against him but this spelling, like 'countrie, flye, manie' and 'mony', may be an alternative of B's. On balance, this evidence favours the thesis that Crane prepared the copy for Wiv.

The evidence of the variants in B's 5½ pages of MM is not conclusive. The 81 B spellings or variants confirm that he was correctly identified as the compositor of $F5^V$, 6, Gla, 1^V, 2^V and G3, and 30 variant spellings remain after nine possible justified spellings have been set aside. However, only eleven of these appear on the Crane spelling list: 'iest, o/oh, powre' and 'yeere/s' are the most significant spellings. Twelve of the remaining spellings show variation of '-ie/y'. There is no information about Crane's spelling of 'contrary', but he strongly preferred '-oo-' in 'bloody', and 'curtesie' and 'murder' for which B tended to reproduce the spellings of his copy, and variants of these words tell against Crane's share in the copy for MM.[100]

The test of B's copy-reflecting spellings has provided some confirmation of Crane's share in some of the

comedies but it has not been as useful as I had hoped.[101]
The words for which B's spellings are known are still too
few, and variants of them are too infrequent in the
comedies for the evidence that has been gathered to be
entirely convincing, and the likelihood of compositorial
variation of the numerous words ending in '-ie/y' on the
list of B's copy-reflecting spellings is too great to
allow confidence in a test which depends largely on such
spellings. This, and B's absence from the composition of
TGV, make it necessary to study the spellings of the early
comedies in another way.

Dr. J. W. Lever has suggested that 'the presence of
a number of spellings which are rare or entirely absent
from the Folio outside this group of plays, though consistently used in the identified transcripts' is good
evidence of the common origin of their copy from Crane's
pen.[102] He noticed that 'sirha', 'misterie', 'ceizes'
and 'midle' (which occurs only twice in Crane's transcripts) were rare outside the plays with which Crane has
been associated. This is patently a good test so long
as a sufficient number of such spellings can be found and
care is taken to exclude the possibility that the spellings
are compositorial. There are many spellings common to the
Folio compositors and Crane, and for most of them there
were no alternative spellings at this time. There is no
advantage in listing their occurrence in the comedies.
Nor is advantage to be expected from study of anomalous
or interesting spellings in the comedies if Crane's
spelling of those words is unknown. I have therefore
selected spellings from the Crane spelling list which
seemed not to be characteristic of spellings in the Folio,

and I have examined their occurrence in the early comedies. Spellings likely to have been affected by justification or other spellings which occurred so frequently as to have been common to Crane and the Folio compositors were set apart. The later comedies were then inspected for these spellings or alternative spellings and again, spellings of which there were no occurrences in the later comedies, or which were common in both groups of texts were discarded. The not-unexpectedly sparse results of this examination are provided below in two tables. The first shows the distribution of characteristic Crane spellings in the early comedies where there were other, presumably compositorial, alternative spellings. With few exceptions, these spellings do not occur in the later comedies.

CRANE SPELLINGS IN THE COMEDIES

Spelling	Tmp.	TGV	Wiv.	MM	WT	Total	Comments
altogeathers			1j			1j	
bruizd			1j			1j	
ceazed		1				1	
ceizes				1		1	
cohear'd				1		1	
confes'd				2		2	
contemning		1				1	contemned TN
councellor	1	1				2	
councels					1	1	
creadit				1		1	
dride			1j			1j	
encreasing	1					1	
extreame		1				1	
fowre	1		2j			1:2	LLL 1j
frend	1					1	TN 1j frends 2j
happely				1		1	
guifts		1				1	Shr. 1j
holly (holy)	1		1j			1:1	
humaine	1					1	

(cont.

CRANE SPELLINGS IN THE COMEDIES (cont.)

Spelling	Tmp.	TGV	Wiv.	MM	WT	Total	Comments
iealouzies			1j			1j	
masque/s		1		1		2	
midle				1		1	
misterie				2:3		2:3	
physick					1	1	
powrefull					2	2	
sirha	2	3:1	1:2	3:2		9:5	
waytes	1					1	
wayting					1	1	
wilbe		1				1	
writt		1				1	
Total	9	11:1	1:9	13:5	5	30:5	

There are other spellings which occur more frequently in the later comedies. Sometimes, like 'dide', they occur only in a single text, sometimes, like 'moneth/s', the frequency of their occurrence in the later comedies seems attributable to justification.

OTHER POSSIBLY SIGNIFICANT SPELLINGS IN THE COMEDIES

Spelling	Tmp.	TGV	Wiv.	MM	WT	Total	Comments
councell			2:3		2	4:3	AWW 1:1 TN 1
daunce	1j				1	1:1	Ado. 1 and dauncer/daunct
dide		1		3		4	TN 4
encrease				1j		1j	AWW 1:1
extreames					1	1	Shr. 1 and extreamely
flowre		1	1	1	1	4	TN 1 and flower/s throughout
flowres	1		2		7	10	LLL 1j TN 1 (cont.

OTHER POSSIBLY SIGNIFICANT SPELLINGS IN THE COMEDIES (cont.)

Spelling	Tmp.	TGV	Wiv.	MM	WT	Total	Comments
gon	2	6	2j	2:1		10:3	gone 39:14; gon 6:1, gone 72:16
graunt	1			2		3	Ado. 1 MND 1j AYL 1j
howre	1	3:1	3j	2:1	1	7:5	10:4
howres	1:1	1	2j	1j		2:4	Err. 2 Shr. 1.
moneth/s		1	1j		4:1	5:2	Ado. 1j LLL 1j MV 1 TN 1j
powr'd				1	1		AYL 1j
publique				2	1	3	LLL 1j AYL 1
seauen		1	2j	1		2:2	MV 2 TN 1j
showre/s	1		1j		1:1		MND 1
Total	8:2	13:2	5:13	11:4	20:1	67:22	

Dr. Lever further suggested that words ending in '-nes' which Crane favoured may also indicate his influence on texts where '-nesse' was the usual spelling. Only 17 of the 85 words in the early comedies which might have ended with '-nes' have that spelling. A table shows the frequency of these words in the five comedies.

SPELLINGS ENDING IN -NES AND -NESSE IN THE
EARLY COMEDIES

	Tmp.	TGV	Wiv.	MM	WT	Total
- NES	4:5	2j	5j	4:2	4j	8:18
- NESSE	32:1	16	2:12	36:10	54:20	140:43

I doubt that this evidence can support the view that Crane prepared the copy for these plays.[103]

Notwithstanding that not all the evidence is
equally valuable, there is substantial confirmation of
the common opinion that the early comedies were printed
from Crane transcripts. Were this the only benefit from
this investigation I could not avoid some disappointment.
However, from time to time indications have been seen
that although the copy for these texts came from a
single hand, it was not uniform in character. It is
possible, moreover, to examine in greater detail the
indications of his influence on individual texts with
confidence that it is indeed to be found and that the
peculiarities observed in these texts are not merely
compositorial. I propose to discuss Tmp., TGV, Wiv.,
MM and WT separately in the next chapter, where, although
I shall be able to take but little account of the character
of the copy which underlies Crane's transcripts, I hope
to show where his influence is to be found.

5. THE FIVE COMEDIES: CONCLUSION

Most attention in this final chapter will be given to particular indications of Crane's influence in the five comedies. These are mainly accidentals, features of orthography in which compositors were not required to follow their copy, although they often allowed them to influence their habits in individual texts. Notice need no longer be taken of purely typographical matters like the arrangement of the dialogue on the page for which the compositors were almost wholly responsible, although some accidentals have been useful to demonstrate the likelihood that Crane prepared transcripts for the five comedies. Nor, without a more detailed examination of the substantives than I can supply at the moment, can reliable estimates be made of the amount of textual corruption in these texts and the responsibility for it, respectively, of the original manuscript, Crane, and the Folio compositors. Dover Wilson remarked 'corruption here and there ... by a copyist [is] of all agents the most difficult to detect or bring to book. An editor can do little more than register his suspicions and pass on.'[104] Occasionally, the possibility of Crane's responsibility for an error can be suggested, but the text of the five comedies cannot be thoroughly studied until appropriate allowance can be made for the habits of the compositors who set them in type.

CONCLUSION

It would be helpful if knowledge of Crane's methods assisted editors to discover the characteristics of the manuscripts from which his transcripts were made. Discussion of this matter is inseparable from discussion of Crane's influence in the five comedies, to which, in order of the texts in the Folio, I now turn.

THE TEMPEST

The frequency and some unusual uses of apostrophes and hyphens are good testimony of Crane's transcription of the copy for Tmp. Particularly significant are apostrophes which denote the omission of a notional word like 'God' of which many more instances are found in the five comedies than in the later comedies. The inference seems justified that the compositors were prepared to follow their copy in this, and that the copy for the later comedies was not characterised by such uses of the apostrophe.[105] The possibility that some of these expressions show Crane's interference with the text cannot be ignored. The New Arden editor represents 'with' King' at 1. 74 clumsily with Grant White's reading, 'wi'th' King', on the ground that the Folio reading 'probably indicates that the author, followed exactly by the printer, wrote with his mind on the words as they would be spoken in haste'.[106] Be this as it may, Crane is more likely than the author to have contributed the apostrophe. Other marks of his punctiliousness may be seen in 'at' nostrils' (1104) and in "'Saue" (847) where the apostrophe indicates the omission of 'God'. On the other hand, nothing is omitted before "'Twentie" (977) and compositor B was probably responsible for the misprint: he had set "'Twould' in the previous line, and "'twixt" occurs in the next.[107] Apostrophes with expressions like "'pray thee" or "'prethee" are also characteristic of Crane's influence, particularly when, as at l. 917, the apostrophe and hyphen are used together. In 'I 'prethee' (1212), the apostrophe is unnecessary: this is less likely to be an indication of a Jonsonian elision than an error. Compositors sometimes made this kind of slip, but other words of this type suggest that for other than the more common words like 'ha's' and 'do's', compositors were prone to omit apostrophes rather than to insert them. There are many instances in Crane's dramatic transcripts of incorrect use of apostrophes of which 'see's' (889) and 'Trinculo's' (1150) are examples from Tmp. On the other hand, the dramatic transcripts offer no instances of his use of apostrophes in 'pow'r' (515, 623), 'pow'rs' (604), and 'pray'r' (569) and compositorial influence must be suspected.

Many of the hyphenated-compounds in Tmp. are of the common varieties noted by Greg, and apart from their relative frequency, they are not unusual. Nouns compounded with adjectives are most common, but there are few instances of verbs compounded with following prepositions or adverbs, which were frequent in his later dramatic transcripts. In the 137 hyphenated-compounds in Tmp., only 'bemockt-at-Stabs' (1596) is of that kind. Compounds with pronouns are also infrequent: 'pre-thee', 'peg-thee' (424) and 'sty-me' (481) are the only instances. In the last two, the hyphen is used to show where metrical stress should fall. Since the large number of hyphens is sufficient to indicate Crane's influence, it is reasonable to suspect that the compositors would not accept many of his more characteristic usages, or that his habits here were not as sophisticated as they were to become when he transcribed Demetrius and Witch. There were few unusual uses of hyphens in compounds in his early transcripts.[108]

Observations that Tmp. was intended to serve 'as a model for the editing' of the Folio depend on two main arguments, that the text was prepared with some degree of care, and that it was the first play to be printed in the Folio.[109] Neither of these arguments will bear inspection. Such signs of 'editorial care' as the division into acts and scenes, the indication of locality and the list of characters in the play, are common in Crane's transcripts, and reveal nothing of his specific intentions for the transcript of Tmp. Nor can it be deduced from these features of the text, or from its accuracy and 'excellent punctuation' that the text itself was given especial attention. The priority of Tmp. in the Folio may probably be attributed to the pleasant appearance of the manuscript as it was originally delivered to the editor or the printer. That it was selected to be printed first in the Folio after it had been prepared is more natural than that it was commissioned to be transcribed in a special way so it could serve as a model. Jaggard would not have started work before most of the copy, at least for the comedies section, was in his hands. Therefore, Crane must already have prepared transcripts of the first few plays. Further, if Tmp. was intended as a model, it cannot have been a good one; TGV and Wiv. have significantly different styles of stage-directions.

If Tmp. was prepared after TGV, Wiv. and MM, for which some evidence may be found, there would have been no point in requiring the scribe to make a special task of the transcript, and he did not accept it as a model for the preparation of his last Folio transcript, WT. In fact, there is no evidence that Crane prepared copy for Tmp. in any special way, and the peculiarities of the other comedies which contrast with Tmp. may be attributed to the influence of his copy on him and to his own variability. However, Pollard's view that the publishers chose a clean manuscript of an unpublished play to introduce the Folio is quite plausible.[110]

The New Arden editor found most support for his elaboration of Greg's opinion in 'the unusually elaborate stage directions' of Tmp. which, he wrote, have no parallel 'save perhaps in the later play, Henry VIII'.[111] The fullness of the directions, especially those at 1535-8 and 1805-8 which describe masque-like features of the action, undoubtedly derives from the copy, which, according to Greg, was foul papers. There are many points of similarity between the directions of Tmp. and those of the other late compositions, H8, Per., Cym. and WT. But the language of the directions, if the directions of his Game transcripts are relevant, probably owes much to him. His interference with the text of the directions may have been even greater if, as Greg suggested, he had seen the play and had incorporated his impressions of the action in the phrasing of the directions.[112]

There is general agreement, although not without some circularity of reasoning, that Crane's transcript was from foul papers. There is no evidence of directions added by the book-keeper to aid production, and the literary character of the descriptive stage-directions, despite Crane's influence on details, shows the hand of the author. Crane did not compose stage-directions himself, unprompted by his copy, nor did he omit them, save when he adopted the convention of massed entrances, to which the directions of <u>Tmp</u>. do not conform. The directions must therefore be substantially the author's, with some embellishment, perhaps stimulated by recent performance of the play, and revision of the language by Crane.[113]

The New Arden editor lists several passages which are mislined in the Folio and where verse is printed as prose, and prose, particularly Caliban's speeches, printed as verse.[114] Some of this here and in the other comedies can surely be attributed to the compositors who were sometimes obliged to make or lose space in order to fit the text into the space allowed for it when the copy was cast-off. No other explanation is necessary for the running together of two lines at the foot of A4 by compositor B. The considerations which apply in particular instances require close examination. Compositor C cannot be held solely responsible for the mislineation on A2^v, for instance, for there are two internal entrances printed to the right of the dialogue, and a speech set on the same line as another line of dialogue which could have been set so as to take up space. Crane's habitual use of minuscules at the beginning of lines, mingled with emphasis capitals, might well have obscured the distinction of prose and verse at some points, and the compositors could have been further confused by the extent to which the text filled the page, without clear distinction of long verse lines and passages of prose. It is safe to assume that much of the mislineation and incorrect setting of verse and prose can be explained by reference to the printing and the characteristics of Crane's transcripts; resort to theories of revision, abridgement, and marginal insertions should not be made until these influences have been allowed for.

The text of Tmp. is generally commended for its comparative absence of detectable error. The Arden editor admits only twenty emendations to the text, of such unexceptional character that extensive discussion is not required.[115]

TEMPEST: READINGS ACCEPTED BY THE NEW ARDEN EDITOR

Page	Comp.	Line	Folio	New Arden	Source
A1	B	30	present	presence	J. C. Maxwell
		66	wide-chopt-rascall	wide-chapp'd-rascal	Cambr.
		77-8	Browne | firrs	broome, furze	Tannenbaum
A2	C	313	Lightning	lightnings	Theobald
		315	sight out-running	sight-outrunning	Cambr.
A2^V	C	409	he	she	Rowe.
A3^V	B	711	Seb.	Ant.	Grant White
		712	Ant.	Seb.	" "
A5^V	A(F)	1250	busie lest	busilest	New Arden (Bulloch)
B1	A(F)	1553	Islands	islanders	F2
		1614	hearts-sorrow	heart-sorrow	Cambr.
B1^V	A(F)	1665	guest	gift	Rowe
		1734	many-coloured	many-colour'd	Rowe
					(cont.

TEMPEST: READINGS ACCEPTED BY THE NEW ARDEN EDITOR (cont.)

Page	Comp.	Line	Folio	New Arden	Source
B2	C	1771	Earths	Cer. Earths	Theobald
		1855	filthy mantled	filthy-mantled	Cambr.
B2^V	C	1906	let's	let't	Rann
		1963	Him that you	Him you	New Arden
		2016	boile	boil'd	Rowe
B3	C	2028	Did (CW Didst)	Didst	
		2031	entertaine	entertain'd	F2

Few of the errors may confidently be laid to Crane's charge. The common 'd/e' misreadings at 2016 and 2031 are probably compositorial, for it is not true that it is 'virtually impossible to confuse "d" and "e" in Crane'.[116] Together with the 'd' with the heavily-written downstroke that is a mark of his hand (the last of the five 'd's illustrated by McKerrow), he also used the commoner closed form which was often misread as 'e'.[117] 'Guest' for 'gift' at 1665 is also probably a misreading; Crane's preferred spelling was 'guift'. More revealing of Crane's influence may be 'present' at l. 30 for which J. C. Maxwell conjectured the reading 'presence'. This is supported by Crane's misreading of 'attendance' at l. 2742 of Demetrius as 'Attendants', but it is even more likely to have been his misreading of the author's 'presenc'.[118] The capital in 'Browne | firrs' at 77-8 suggests that the misreading was more probably Crane's than the compositor's, and the spelling 'firrs' is undoubtedly his, but most of the errors are so trivial that it is difficult to determine the respective responsibility of the scribe and the compositors. The small number of errors which have been detected gives some indication of the care with which copy for Tmp. was transcribed, but it supplies little information about Crane's fidelity to the substantives of his copy.[119]

The paucity of metrical variants is worthy of mention. There are a fair number of 'will' elisions of which Crane's spelling was conventional, and four 'would' elisions of which he was more apt to vary the spelling, but, apart from 'I'am' at 1. 64, there is no indication that copy for Tmp. contained Jonsonian elisions. Since Crane did not favour their use before 1624, it is probably true that there were not many in his transcript for if they had been present, with or without apostrophes, and the compositors had omitted to set the apostrophe, the metre would have been affected. The New Arden edition records 'you have' (82) as 'a weak ending' and notes conjectures of 'I've' for 'I have' at 351 and 1184 by Pope and Dyce respectively. Capell's emendation 'you've' in 'you'r paid' at 712 is not attractive because Crane did not use that spelling of the elision in his dramatic transcripts, but there is some foundation for his reading of 'she'd' in 'should bow' (805) in Crane's spelling 'she'll'd'.[120] None of these readings was accepted by the New Arden editor.

TWO GENTLEMEN OF VERONA

There is little to say about TGV of which the most significant characteristic is the massed entrances and all but complete suppression of directions for action within scenes.[121] There are exits at 66, 203, 525 and 845, and at the ends of all the scenes except 4.2 (1764), doubtless an oversight, but there are no descriptive directions like those of **Tmp**. at all. Crane did not suppress all the descriptive directions in **Game** Malone which also has massed entries, so it is likely that the stage-directions of his copy were scanty; modern editors have not added more than a few 'aside's, 'she reads's and the like. Greg's view was that Crane copied a playhouse manuscript because the massed entrances supply, after their fashion, correct entries for all the characters of the play.[122] It is unreasonable to expect that they would not. Indications of production, directions for music and properties, are absent. Crane may have edited them out of his copy, but there is no evidence that the King's Men supplied him with their prompt-books. The New Arden editor maintains the contrary opinion that his copy was foul papers and lists numerous inconsistencies and obscurities of nomenclature, plot and characterisation which, he considered, would not have survived in a prompt copy. He found two stages of composition which resulted in a composite draft which Crane could have prepared for the printer. The balance of probabilities seems to favour Professor Leech's conclusion. The question of why he chose the massed kind of entrance is not readily answerable. His choice is rather more explicable if his copy was fragmentary and required editorial attention before transcription, but in the nature of things, one cannot be certain of this.[123]

Particular uses of the apostrophe are characteristic of Crane's habits and confirm his influence even though apostrophes are less frequent in TGV than in three of the other texts for which he transcribed copy. The early date of the play may have significance for the number of the apostrophes. Apostrophes indicate the omission of notional words in "'saue" (74), "'foole" (207), which probably shows sophistication of the text, "'giue ye-good-ev'n" (490), an expression most typical of his orthography, and "'pox" (1440). Other characteristic uses of apostrophes occur in 'with'em' (1546), 'about'ye' (1547) where the apostrophe is redundant,[124] and in seven instances of possessive singulars of proper nouns after vowels.

Hyphenated compounds are also relatively infrequent; the language of the play must partly have contributed to this. Hyphenation of common prefixes as in 'ore-look'd' and 'vn-welcome' occurs quite often but is probably not especially significant of Crane's influence. There are few of the kinds of compound which Greg noticed. Prepositions or adverbs are compounded with verbs in 'come-on', 'falls-off', 'hardly-off', and 'stand-vnder', and there is one hyphenated pronoun, 'rest-them', where the hyphen appears to emphasize what is the normal stress of a monosyllabic verb followed by a pronoun. Most of the compounds are hyphenated adjectives and nouns. Nevertheless, the frequency of compounds is consistent with Crane's influence on the text.

The small number of emendations which the New Arden editor admitted to his text shows that it was accurately

CONCLUSION 115

transcribed and printed, although, considering the readings set out below and the errors of Crane's other transcripts, there may well be other trivial errors which have escaped detection. It is difficult to assign responsibility for the misreadings, substitutions, and small omissions of words and letters to Crane or the compositors, although the readings of the uncorrected formes of TGV which survive go some way to demonstrate the influence of compositors.

TWO GENTLEMEN: READINGS ACCEPTED BY THE NEW ARDEN EDITOR[125]

Page	Comp.	Line	Folio	New Arden	Source
B4^V	A(F)	69	loue	leave	Pope
		81	I Sheepe?	I a sheep?	F2
B5	A(F)	143	cestern'd	testerned	F2
		207	'foole	fool	F4
B5^V	A(F)	256	you	your	F2
		273	Loue wounded	love-wounded	F2
		281	fearefull, hanging	fearful-hanging	Delius
B6	C	352	Pro. Oh	O	F2
		378	Panthmo	Panthino	
		379		Exit Antonio and Panthino.	F2
		390	Fathers call's	father calls	F2 subst.
B6^V	C	584		Exit Julia.	Rowe
C1^V	C	736		Exit.	Rowe
		767	Thur.	Ser.	Theobald
		772		Exeunt Silvia, Thurio, Speed and Servant.	Capell
		820	make	makes	F2
		851	It is mine	Is it mine eye	Malone
C2	C	865	dazel'd	dazeled	New Arden
		870	Exeunt.	Exit.	F2
C2^V	C	1071		Exit Thurio.	Rowe

(cont.)

TWO GENTLEMEN: READINGS ACCEPTED BY THE NEW ARDEN EDITOR
(cont.)

Page	Comp.	Line	Folio	New Arden	Source
C3	C	1119		Exit.	Rowe
C3^v	C	1238		Exit.	F2
		1290	banish'd	banished	Pope
		1328		Exeunt Proteus and Valentine.	F2
C4	A(F)	1440		Exit.	Capell
		1443	Exeunt.	Exit.	Capell
C4^v	A(F)	1494	weede	wind	Keightley
		1579	often had beene often	often had been	F2
		1593	And heire and Neece,	An heir, and near	Theobald
C5	A(F)	1705		Exeunt Thurio and Musicians.	Rowe
C5^v	A(F)	1736	her	his	F2
		1757		Exeunt Protheus and Silvia.	F2
		1764		Exeunt.	F2
C6	A(F)	1873	Hangmans boyes	hangman boys	Singer
		1879		Exit Launce.	F2
		1887	know thee	know thou	F2
		1891	not leaue	to leave	F2
		1908		Exit.	F2
C6^v	A(F)	1996		Exit.	F2
		2023	Exeunt.	Exit.	F2
		2071	saw Eglamoure	saw Sir Eglamour	F4
		2090		Exit.	Rowe
		2094		Exit.	Capell
		2096		Exit.	Capell
		2098	Exeunt.	Exit.	Capell
D1	C	2111		Exeunt 2 and 3 Outlaws.	Capell
		2190	trusted	trusted now	F2

There are no Jonsonian apostrophes in TGV and the New Arden editor noted only one other emendation of an elision which would improve the metre, Pope's suggestion of 'I've' in 'Already haue I bin' at 1623.

MERRY WIVES OF WINDSOR

The marks of Crane's influence are particularly strong in <u>Wiv</u>. of which the colloquial language gave many opportunities for his use of apostrophes, hyphens and parentheses. He was sometimes indifferent to the use of hyphens and apostrophes to separate constituent parts of words, as 'pre'thee' and 'pre-thee' in the dramatic transcripts illustrate, and there are instances of this in <u>Wiv</u>.: "'o-man/o'man/s", 'adowne'a', 'giue-'a', 'matter'a', 'content-a', 'a'shoare', 'quoth'a', 'ore'flowes' and 'procure'a' show this kind of inconsistency. 'Ver'is' is a Jonsonian elision, and apostrophes denote the omission of notional words in "'faith, 'blesse, 'pleases, 'saue, 'giue, 'pray, 'blessing" and "'vengeance". This text also has apostrophes with possessives after consonants in 'go't's, got's, got's-will, od's, odd's-hart-lings, od's-nownes", and to indicate peculiarities of speech in 'the'ord' and 'watch'ords' and some of the previous terms. This is very characteristic of Crane at his fussiest and the compositors cannot be supposed to be responsible.

There are 311 occurrences of hyphenated-compounds, a number which is approached only by <u>WT</u>. They resemble the compounds of the later literary transcripts more closely than the compounds of the other Folio comedies in the variety of ways in which the hyphen is used. Verbs compounded with pronouns or with adverbs or prepositions are too numerous to list in full: instances are 'awe-him, carry-her, come-on, drawes-on' and 'mary-her'. Hyphenation of articles with nouns and similar constructions imparts a fluid rhythm to the colloquial speeches. One can only guess how many, if any at all, of the hyphens in compounds like 'clapper-de-claw, des-toyes, fery-well, indeede-la, let-a-mee, littell-a-while, make-a-de-sot, make-a-the, no-come, no-the, peace-a-your, speake-a-your, take-a-your' and 'tell-a-me' existed in the copy for Crane's transcript. The variety and number of compounds leaves no reasonable doubt of his influence on this text. However, it should be noticed that the style and the fact that the greater part of Wiv. is prose has probably influenced his use of hyphens, just as the amount of prose gives greater weight to the relative frequency of apostrophes (lowest of the five comedies) in this text. These observations, together with the high proportion of parentheses, would support a case that the Folio text was printed from Crane's transcript of his own earlier transcript, were other evidence of this to be found.

The survival of the memorially reconstructed first quarto of 1602 aids emendation of passages which are obscure in the Folio, but Crane's strong influence, particularly the massed entrances and suppression of all but one of the necessary internal entries and of other descriptive stage-directions, makes it difficult to determine the nature of the copy which he transcribed. The Cambridge editors, who knew nothing of Crane, thought that the Folio text 'was probably printed from a carelessly written copy of the author's MS.'[126] Greg's earliest view was the 'the folio (save for minor errors) does faithfully represent the full authoritative text current in the playhouse at the date of publication.'[127] He later concluded that the purging of oaths and the substitution of Broome for Q1's Brooke as Ford's pseudonym, implied access to the prompt-book, in which such necessary alterations must have been marked.[128] The question of Crane's copy is complicated by evidence of revision of the incident of the stealing of the Host's horses and of certain passages of the fifth act for which the quarto and folio present different versions. These alterations too, in Greg's opinion, were probably added to the prompt-book for subsequent performance. He did not examine the possibility that the Folio version of the fifth act was preserved with the author's papers, or that Crane's transcript was checked against the prompt-book in the knowledge that it contained alterations which at the least it was inadvisable to omit from a text printed in the Folio. These considerations and the absence of any sure indications that Crane copied the prompt-book lend some weight to the likelihood that his copy was foul papers. More shall be said of this later.[129]

Even with the help of the quarto, the Cambridge editors found little occasion to correct the text. Some phrases were introduced from the quarto, mostly without justification in Greg's view, and some 'oaths' were reintroduced, but in the main the text is fairly free from substantial error, as the Cambridge collations and the readings that they admitted into the text show. The New Arden editor made less use of Q and retained F's euphemisms, and found no more occasion than the Cambridge editors to emend the text.

MERRY WIVES: READINGS ACCEPTED BY THE NEW ARDEN EDITOR

Page	Comp.	Line	Folio	New Arden	Source
D2	C	61	Slen.	Shal.	Capell
D3	A(F)	314	liue	lime	Q(lyme)
		346	a legend	a legion	Rowe[3]
		351	illiads	œillades	Hanmer, conj. Pope
D3^V	A(F)	438	vnboyteene verd	une boitine verde	Craig
		444	mai foy, il fait for ehando, le man voi a le Court la grand affaires	ma foi, il fait fort chaud. Je m'en vais voir à la court la grande affaire	New Arden
		460	La-roone	laroon	Rowe
D4	C	554	haue scap'd	have I scaped	Q3
D4^V	C	603	praise	praised	Theobald
D5	C	744	Shal.	Ford	Q
		746	Broome	Brook (throughout)	Q
D6^V	C	1118	a Mounseur	A word Mounseur	Q
E1	B	1250	No-verbes	add: Give me thy hand, terrestrial, so	Q; as Theobald
		1254	Lad	lads	Q
		1364	Dotchet Mead	Datchet Mead	As Rowe
E2	B	1522	foolishion	foolish	F2
		1581	No	Fent. No	Q3
E2^V	B	1635	Fenter	Fenton	Q3
E3^V	B	1957	Mist.Ford.	Mrs. Page	Malone
		1992	misuse enough	misuse him enough	F2
		2001	liefe as	as lief	F2
		2006	gin	ging	F2
E4	B	2064	him strike	him not strike	Q3
		2117	houses	house	Q
		2129	gold	cold	Rowe
E4^V	B	2155	make	makes	F2

(cont.

MERRY WIVES: READINGS ACCEPTED BY THE NEW ARDEN EDITOR
(cont.)

Page	Comp.	Line	Folio	New Arden	Source
E5	A(F)	2184	Ford.	Mrs. Ford	Rowe
		2261	Fal.	Sim.	Rowe
		2306	Huy	Hue	Rowe
		2307	huy	hue	Rowe
		2382	deuote	denote	Capell, conj. Steevens
E5ᵛ	B	2421	Goliah	Goliath	Steevens[3]
		2434	my	my daughter	F2
		2459	Herne	Hugh	Capell
E6	B	2547	Nightly-meadow-Fairies	nightly, meadow-fairies	As Capell
		2553	Saphire-pearle	sapphire, pearl	Theobald
E6ᵛ	B	2682	greene	white	Rowe[3]
		2686	white	green	Rowe[3]
		2690	con pesant	un paysan	As Capell
		2692	white	green	Pope

There are many minim errors but it is not possible to be sure whether Crane was in error or the compositors experienced difficulty in reading his transcript: sometimes words lack minims in his script, but this is not peculiar to his hand. The omission of a phrase at 1250 seems to indicate an eye skip on account of 'Celestiall' which follows, but again, the compositor is as likely as Crane to have been at fault. Omissions at 1992, 2064 and 2434 which could have been supplied had they been noted in the compositor's copy point to carelessness on B's part, and there are other omissions by C at 554 and 1118. Crane is more likely to have been responsible for the errors at 2547 and 2553, but it can hardly be said that the signs of his influence on the substantives of Wiv. are clear.[130]

MEASURE FOR MEASURE

The text of MM has recently been rehabilitated by the New Arden editor, J. W. Lever, whose conclusion that 'Behind some slapdash work in the printing house, and a number of scribal idiosyncrasies, stands Shakespeare's own rough draft in reasonably good condition' finds ready assent.[131] Substantial textual anomalies which some editors have taken to indicate revision, are certain signs of foul papers, and although the critical problems of MM are well known, its principal textual deficiencies and inconsistencies are not of the kind for which compositors or scribe should be held responsible. Nevertheless, the influence of these agents on particular points of textual significance is sometimes conspicuous, and the task of determining what features of the text should be laid to the charge of author, scribe and compositors respectively is more than usually complicated by the division of the printing amongst four compositors.[132]

The stage-directions are mostly limited to necessary entrances and exits. As directions like 'Enter Duke ... Citizens at seuerall doores' (5.1) are consistent with Shakespeare's directions elsewhere, and as Crane did not usually omit descriptive directions unless he was using the convention of massed entrances, it is reasonable to assume that only the most necessary directions were present in his copy. The style of the directions is, in fact, consistent with those in TGV although that text, unlike MM, has massed entries. It is pointless to consider too closely why the same convention was not adopted for MM; perhaps the greater diversity and complexity of the movements of the characters within scenes influenced the scribe to retain the directions of his copy.[133] The omission of about twenty exits should not be laid to Crane's charge: nearly all of them are clearly indicated by the dialogue or provide for the obvious movements of servants, attendants and other minor characters. Probably these exits were not marked in the foul papers.

The New Arden editor's observation that internal entries 'are where an author would place them - immediately before the new character speaks or is addressed in the dialogue - and not where they might appear in prompt-copy, a few lines ahead as advance notice to the actors' does not take account of Crane's habits.[134] All interior entrances in his dramatic transcripts were written to the right of dialogue, and were not centered or otherwise conspicuously marked. It has already been seen that because he inserted them after writing the dialogue, they could be misplaced. At the least, the compositors, who often centered entrances within a scene on the width of the column, could mistake the correct place for their insertion.[135] The misplaced entrances for Isabella on $F5^v$ (1248) and Lucio on G1 (1529) are probably instances of this. Similarly, Crane's practice with 'within' directions was to write 'within' after the speech-prefix when the dialogue was to be spoken off-stage (e.g. 'Boy wthin', Barnavelt 1671) or alongside the dialogue at the right when the direction was for off-stage noises. 'Noice within' in Game Lansdowne and Malone 649, and 'Alarum | within' in Demetrius 1778 show his practice. The three centered 'within' directions which Greg noticed as 'unusual and perhaps confined to this play',[136] are paralleled by 'Cry within' on I1^v of Err., which was set, together with two of the same directions of MM, by compositor B. His tendency to centre marginal directions casts doubt on the influence of copy here: the compositors were almost certainly responsible.

The emendations which the New Arden editor admitted to his text show the familiar mixture of omissions, transpositions and misreadings for which it is difficult to decide responsibility with any confidence.

MEASURE FOR MEASURE: READINGS ACCEPTED BY THE NEW ARDEN EDITOR

Page	Comp.	Line	Folio	New Arden	Source
F1a	C	18		Exit an Attendant.	Capell
F1b	D	84	Exit.	to after line 85	F2
F2a	C	225	mortality	morality	Rowe
F2b	D	310	weedes	jades	New Arden
F2^v	C	353	Sisterstood	sisters stood	New Arden
		463	our	your	Rowe
F3^v	C	657		Exit Froth.	Rowe
		718		Exit Elbow.	Rowe
F4	C	734		Exit Servant.	Capell
		756		Enter Servant.	Capell
		763		Exit Servant.	Theobald
F4^v	C	868	neuer	ne're	F2
		920	prayers crosse	prayer's cross'd	New Arden

(cont.

MEASURE FOR MEASURE: READINGS ACCEPTED BY THE NEW ARDEN
EDITOR   (cont.)

Page	Comp.	Line	Folio	New Arden	Source
		924		Exeunt all but Angelo.	Alexander
F5a	C	1011	feard	sere	Hudson
		1019		Knock.	New Arden
		1021		Exit Servant.	Capell
F5b	D	1057	and	or	Rowe
		1102	all-building-Law	all-binding-law	Johnson
F5ᵛ	B	1232	fire	sire	F4
F6	B	1248	Enter Isabella.	Is. [Within]	Capell
		1254		Enter Isabella.	Dyce
		1280	Through	Though	Rowe
		1305	emmew	enew	Keightley
		1309	prenzie	precise	Knight
		1311	damnest	damnedst	F2
		1312	prenzie gardes	precise guards	Knight
		1349	periury	penury	F2
F6ᵛ	C	1468	time... place	place...time	Ridley
		1473	heere	hear	New Arden
		1498	Foxe and	fox on	Rann
G1a	B	1514	away	array	Theobald
		1529	Enter Lucio.	to after line 1530	Alexander
G1b	D	1600	generatiue	ungenerative	Theobald
G1ᵛ	B	1692		Exeunt Officers with Mistress Overdone.	Dyce
		1700	Good'euen	Good even	F4
		1710	as it is as	it is as	F3
		1744		Exit Escalus and Provost.	New Arden
		1759-60		[2 lines omitted]	New Arden
G2a		1777		Exit Boy.	Malone
G2b		1828	and haue	so have	New Arden
G2ᵛ	B	1897	Clo. If	If	Capell

(cont.

MEASURE FOR MEASURE: READINGS ACCEPTED BY THE NEW ARDEN EDITOR (cont.)

Page	Comp.	Line	Folio	New Arden	Source
		1925		Exit Claudio.	Capell
		2009	wreaklesse	reckless	Pope
G3	B	2093	Shootie	Shoe-tie	Steevens
G3^V	B	2146		Exeunt Abhorson and Pompey.	Capell
		2172	yond	yonder	Rowe
		2183	weale-ballanc'd	well-balanc'd	New Arden
		2241	Good'euen	Good even	Rowe
		2251		Exit Isabella.	Theobald
G4a	C	2277	re-|liuer	redeliver	Capell
		2297	of a	so	New Arden
		2313	Flauia's	Flavius'	Pope
		2318		Exit Friar.	Theobald
G4b	A(F)	2361	we your	we our	New Arden
		2385	heere	hear	Neilson
G5	C	2541	your	her	F2
		2593	promis'd	promised	Rowe
		2631		Exit an Attendant.	New Arden
		2648		Exit an Attendant.	Dyce
G6a	A(F)	2812	confutation	confiscation	F2
		2866		Exit Provost.	Hanmer
G6^V	C	2938	that	that's	F2
		2938		Exeunt omnes.	Rowe

Compositor C could have set 'mortality' for 'morality' at 225 but Crane is just as likely to have been in error. 'Sisterhood' was probably not misprinted, for the 'h' and the 'st' ligature were in separate cases of the divided lay in use at the time, but the 'st' sort might have been incorrectly distributed. The New Arden reading 'sisters stood' is cacophonous. The much

discussed crux at 493, 'brakes of Ice', probably shows
assimilation of 'f' and 'v' as the line was carried in the
mind but again, scribe or compositor could equally well
have been responsible. If Knight's emendation 'precise'
is correct for 'prenzie', the error was Crane's for his
'z' cannot be misread. The New Arden editor retained
without explanation of its meaning 'th'unsisting' at 1949;
the elided 'th'' is probably Crane's, and if Capell's
conjecture 'unshifting' is correct, the metre demands the
elision. The other conjectures are unattractive. The
correct reading might be discovered by comparison with
'sisterstood' at 350, which was set by a different compositor. Compositor C obviously misprinted 'redeliver'
but Crane, who was apt to omit terminal letters, is as
likely as B to have truncated 'yonder' at 2172. Nevertheless, the number of errors in B's share of MM is
probably significant. Crane's hand writing was not
responsible for the errors at 1057 ('and/or'), 1498
('and/on') and 1828 ('and/so/oft'); these were transmitted from his copy, as his ampersand, which he did not
use frequently in the dialogue, cannot be mistaken for
the words suggested. His copy was also responsible for
the error 'weedes' at 310 for which the New Arden
reading 'jades' is attractive. There is a similar error
in TGV at 1494.

'Good'euen' at 1700 and 2241 shows Crane's variation
of hyphen and apostrophe: the hyphenated form is more
common in his dramatic transcripts. Such expressions may
change colloquialisms in his copy which editors should be
prepared to restore in appropriate circumstances. Other
uses of apostrophes which show his influence are

'pray'thee, pre'thee, 'faith, 'pray, 'saue, 'please,
'fore-noone, 'blesse' and the Jonsonian apostrophe in
'I'haue' (1206). There are also ten instances of
apostrophes with possessive singulars of nouns ending in
vowels. None of the emendations necessary to mend the
metre reveals sure error on Crane's part.

There are instances of adverbs or prepositions
compounded with verbs, as 'giuing-out, Keepe-downe,
run-by' and 'tyde-vp' but no verb-pronoun compounds.
In MM, most of the hyphenated-compounds are of the
common adjective-noun kind, or hyphenated prefixes and
stems for which sometimes the compositors may have been
responsible. Although the 87 hyphenated-compounds in MM
are adequate witness to Crane's influence, this text
has the least number of the five early comedies: they
are more frequent in LLL. Nevertheless, the evidence of
Crane's share in the preparation of copy for MM is
ample enough.

THE WINTER'S TALE

The last of the five comedies is WT, in which there
is good evidence of Crane's influence in the lavish
hyphens, apostrophes and parentheses. A thorough examination of the typography and orthography by J. H. P.
Pafford leaves little scope for further observations on
these matters and detailed discussion here is not
necessary.[137] The uses of hyphens in metrical compounds
like 'auouch-it' is consistent with Crane's practice in
Pleasure[138] and there are many instances of verbs compounded with pronouns, and prepositions or adverbs. Other

occurrences of hyphens in compounds, which, after <u>Wiv</u>.,
are most frequent in this text, add little to those mentioned so far, but the variety of circumstances in
which they occur is strong evidence of Crane's hand. <u>WT</u>
has the greatest relative frequency of apostrophes. They
are used many times to denote omission of letters and of
notional words in expressions like "'Beseech you", 'Who
taught 'this' (600) and 'to bed with'Sun' (1918). The
number of these probably reflects the style of language
of this late composition and certainly shows Crane's close
attention to its orthography. Variation of the hyphen
and apostrophe to separate constituents of compound words
is normal to Crane, and 'Gilly'vors' (1910) should
probably be printed as 'Gilly-vors' (so 1890) by a
modernising editor willing to accept Crane's indications
of orthography. There is a Jonsonian elision in
'Verely'is' (109) and many possessive singulars of nouns
with apostrophes after vowels. The unusual number of
'it's' with the apostrophe (230, 231, 236, 357, 1488)
indicates his influence; the Shakespearian 'it' for the
possessive is also found at 1110 and 1279. It is rather
surprising that 'I'll' does not occur in <u>WT</u> as it does
in <u>MM</u> which must have been transcribed earlier.

The stage-directions contain an interesting mixture
of conventional and massed entries, with a sprinkling of
directions which have a literary flavour. The entries
for 1.1, 1.2, 3.1, 4.1 and 4.2 supply no evidence of
Crane's methods since the characters named in the scene
heading are on stage from the beginning. Two other
scenes, 4.3 and 5.2, have conventional entries at the
appropriate places. There remain eight scenes for which

the characters are listed together in order of their
subsequent entries, at the head of the scene. In four of
these directions (2.1, 3.2, 5.1, 5.3) the groups of
characters which enter later in the scene are separated
by colons. These were all set by compositor A. There
can be no doubt that he reproduced the colons which were
in Crane's transcript, for colons are used in a similar
way in the massed entries of his <u>Game</u> Malone transcript.[139]
Compositor B was apparently unwilling to print the colons
from copy which must have been in the headings to 2.2,
2.3, 3.3 and 4.4. For some of the scenes which have
massed entries there are internal entries for some of the
characters, and three of the fifteen internal entrances
in the scenes which have massed directions provide for
the re-entry of characters listed in the main heading.
This may argue Crane's attention to the action, but this
is contradicted by other evidence. 'Servant' and
'Paulina' are not included in the massed entry for 3.2
and do not have separate entries in the scene, and the
Babe is omitted from the heading to 2.3. The Lord who
has an internal entry at 2940 was also omitted from the
direction to 5.1, unless he was included among the
'Servants'. Some exits are lacking, but this is not
unusual in his transcripts from foul papers.

I earlier argued that Crane made two transcripts
from foul papers, one to replace the prompt-book which
was missing before a new prompt-book was relicensed on
August 19th, 1623, and the other as copy for the Folio.[140]
The cleanness of the text and the sophistication of its
orthography, together with a frequency of parentheses
unusual even in Crane's transcripts, led me to conclude

that the prompt-book was transcribed first, and that the Folio copy was made from the prompt-book, for his characteristics were stronger in transcripts made like Game Lansdowne from his own earlier transcript. This theory, which is not susceptible of conclusive proof, finds further support from the massed entries which would have been out of place in a copy made for use as a prompt-book but which could easily have been compiled from a transcript with conventional entries. Why he should choose massed entries when he had a clean manuscript available is not readily explained, but the variety of the directions argues that the copy was prepared in some haste, under conditions which did not allow the scribe to adopt the massed convention completely. It is known that the printing of the last of the Folio comedies was delayed because copy for WT was not available.

The text, however, so far as its accuracy can be examined from the New Arden collations, has few errors, and many of these are compositorial.

WINTER'S TALE: READINGS ACCEPTED BY THE NEW ARDEN EDITOR

Page	Comp.	Line	Folio	New Arden	Source
Aa1	A	30	hath	have	F2
Aa1^v	A	175	A	And	F2
Aa2	A	237	Ornaments oft do's	Ornaments oft do	Rowe
		290	you say	you they say	F2
Aa2^v	A	368	Holy-Horse	hobby-horse	Rowe
Aa4^v	B	881	le't	let't	
		945	Who	What	F2
Aa5^v	A	1185	Silence.	Silence!	Rowe
Aa6	A	1353	hazard	certain hazard	F2

(cont.

WINTER'S TALE: READINGS ACCEPTED BY THE NEW ARDEN EDITOR

(cont.)

Page	Comp.	Line	Folio	New Arden	Source
Bb1	B	1559	mad	made	New Arden
Bb2	B	1810	Digest with	Digest it with	F2
		1811	sworne	swoon	Theobald
		1843	deer'st	dearest	New Arden
Bb2v	B	1910	you	your	F2
		1980	on't	out	Theobald
Bb3v		2184	whom	who	F2
		2262	acknowledge	acknowledg'd	F2
		2266	whom	who	F2
		2272	shalt neuer	shalt	Rowe
Bb4	B	2283	hope	hoop	Pope
		2316	my	your	F2
		2353	who	whom	F2
Bb5	A	2617	at	or	F2
		2795	(Where... now appear)	(Were...now) appeare	Rann
		2798	iust such	just	F3
Cc1v	A	3302	On	Or	Hanmer
Cc2	B	3334	Viols	vials	Pope

Crane's spelling 'holly' might explain the printing of 'Holy-Horse' for 'hobby-horse', and the setting of 'Silence.' in italic at 1185 is an instance of his use of italic handwriting for emphasis. The New Arden editor, who acknowledged that there 'can be no certainty about the nature of Crane's immediate source', described it as a 'very good text'.[141] There is no sure evidence of this. By the time Crane had copied his source text twice (or, indeed, only once) many of the obscurities of his copy had been smoothed out. The texts of all five comedies have been described by modern editors as 'good', an opinion justified by the small number of errors which have been detected in them. Crane, however, was not prone to write rubbish; the kind of nonsense set up by a baffled compositor in the first quarto of _Lr_. is never found in his transcripts, and even when he may be suspected of error, the reading of his transcript is at the least plausible. If his sophistication of the texts he transcribed had been less, more could be discovered of the nature of his copy. The 'goodness' of _Tmp_., _TGV_, _Wiv_., _MM_, and _WT_ means little more than that the printer's copy was free from obvious error. The general level of Crane's accuracy was high, but he was not reluctant to interfere with his text, consciously or unconsciously, when its meaning was obscure to him. Certainly, there is more of his orthography in these texts than the author's. These considerations should encourage editors to regard the 'correctness' of the texts printed from Crane transcripts with renewed scepticism.

At least one of Crane's dramatic transcripts shows reformation of profanity. The texts of _Demetrius_ and _The Humourous Lieutenant_, as Bald noted, differ. Whereas the manuscript preserves two passages which were probably censored in the printed text, the oaths and asseverations of the transcript were toned down.[142] Terms like 'Lord, Death, Pox' and "'Life" which appear in the folio text printed from the prompt-book are omitted in the transcript. Crane may have taken account of the 'religious inclinations' of Sir Kenelm Digby to whom he dedicated the transcript. He was not as scrupulous in his other transcripts: 'pox', for instance, is used as an oath in _Barnavelt_, _Game_ Folger and _Witch_. Although the language of _Game_, apart from its political references, has been partially reformed, there remain many expressions to which objection might have been made at the time.

When there is no opportunity to compare texts of a play which were printed from different kinds of copy, it is difficult to determine where the responsibility for expurgation of profanity correctly lies. One cannot be sure that the author himself did not choose to use euphemisms. The influence of the Act of Abuses (1606), the tendency of the age to greater decorum of expression, and occasional zealous censorship separately or together may have influenced authors and particular texts to varying extents. Charles and Sir Henry Herbert at a later time did not agree on what were legitimately censorable terms, and expurgation was so desultory that the significance of the absence or presence of oaths in printed texts cannot often be confidently decided. Greg concluded that '...profanity cannot be regarded as affording altogether reliable evidence respecting the nature and date of the manuscript that served as copy for a printed text'.[143]

Addition II of STM shows that Shakespeare used language which was likely to be censored under some circumstances.[144] Comparison of quarto and Folio Wiv. reveals incomplete expurgation of oaths in the Folio text. Evans and Caius were, as Chambers commented, 'hard swearers' in the quarto, and some oaths like 'od's-me' (455) occur in the Folio.[145] But, in the light of Greg's opinion, it cannot be decided whether the language had been incompletely reformed in the manuscripts Crane was given to transcribe, or whether he was instructed to remove offensive expressions. There is no evidence that he would have reformed the language on his own initiative. Alice Walker's view was that 'The removal of profanity from Folio plays was ... editorial in inspiration.'[146] The question of Crane's responsibility for the removal of oaths is open. My own view is that had Crane been given specific instructions to reform the language, he would have performed his task, particularly in <u>Wiv</u>., more thoroughly than he did.

I once thought that it might be possible to explain characteristics of the texts, particularly the massed entries, by reference to the order in which Crane made the transcripts for the Folio. An attempt to determine the order of the transcripts is fraught with uncertainty, and at the moment, not enough is known about the copy from which he transcribed and of the habits of the compositors for it to be possible to arrange the transcripts convincingly. However, there is some encouragement in one of the implications of the present examination. The compositors reproduced more of the orthographical characteristics of their copy, notably apostrophes, hyphenation, capitals and other punctuation, than Moxon's dicta and study of the texts printed from quarto copy have led many scholars to believe. Unless this were true as a general principle, there would be no grounds for the examination of Crane's influence in the Folio. However, the uniform occurrence of characteristics which have been identified as Crane's in the dramatic transcripts in pages set by four (or five) different compositors, and the absence of these orthographical details from other texts set by the same compositors is all the proof that is necessary that they were greatly influenced by their copy.

Lingering doubts are dispelled when the first quarto of <u>Duchess of Malfi</u> (1623) is examined for traces of Crane's influence. There are at least 239 occurrences of hyphens in compounds, of which the most informative of Crane's influence are 'Tilt-often, deadly-dogged, womans-fault, throttle-her, not-Being, Cockatrixes-egge, wifes-voyce, litle-Ones, lying-in, cas'de-vp, mounte-banckes' (with his usual 'nck' spelling), 'faire-ones, Duch-man, Por-pisse' (for 'porpoise'), 'Huntes-man' (see <u>Game</u> Malone, 1849), and hyphens appearing to emphasise metrical stress in 'flie-thee, night-thee, diuine-is' and 'discipline-is' (H2).[147]

There are many familiar elisions, like 'I'll'd, I'l'd, I'ld, you'll'd, youl'd, we'll, wee'll, she'll, they'll', and 'I'll', Crane's later spelling: I have noticed only three 'I'le' spellings. 'Th'hast' for 'thou'st' is probably not Crane's. Apostrophes to show the omission of letters are common: "'gin, 'gins, o'the, neu'r" and "eu'n" (his preferred spellings), "'cause, it's, do's, 'tweene, 'bout, 'boue', ta'ne, h'as (he has), ha's (has)" and "at's" all have been seen in his dramatic transcripts, where also apostrophes to denote omission of notional words were also common. "'Faith" and "'pray" are instances in <u>Duchess of Malfi</u>. 'Prethee' or 'pray thee' appears in a variety of forms: "'pray, 'pray-thee, pre'thee, pre-thee" and 'pray-thee' which, as I have already observed, is quite typical of Crane's habits. There are apostrophes in possessive singulars of nouns in '<u>Pliney</u>'s' (B2^V), 'god's' (G3), 'it's' (K1), '<u>Delio</u>'s' (L4), '<u>Antonio</u>'s' (M3, N2, N3^V) and 'Cardinall's' (M3^V), but there is only one Jonsonian elision, 'here'it'

on E4. Sententia or gnomic expressions may be seen on
fifteen pages, sometimes italicised, sometimes with an
introductory quotation mark, and twice, on N1 and N4,
both italicised and with quotation marks. The two compositors of the 1623 quarto, then, attended to the
orthography of their copy.[148]

On the necessary assumption that the compositors did
not seriously influence the proportions of punctuation in
the five comedies, an attempt to determine the order of
preparation of the copy is assisted by knowledge that
Crane's punctuation and other orthographical characteristics
became heavier between 1618 and 1625.[149] Jonsonian elisions occur too infrequently to assist this examination;
they do not appear to have been used in any number before
the Game transcripts of 1624. Evidence of changes of
spelling habits in the early 1620's is obscured by the
compositors of whose own habits there is not enough known to
enable allowances to be made. The only evidence of order
which may be useful at the moment is the frequency of
punctuation. This suggests that the transcripts were
prepared in the order MM, TGV, Tmp., Wiv. and WT. The
amount of prose in Wiv. affects the use of parentheses and
hyphens and it is more likely, if suitable allowances
could be made, that Wiv. would be found to have been
transcribed before Tmp.; there is little difference between
the proportion of punctuation to words in these two texts.
The only certainty is that WT was the last transcript to
be prepared, and its frequency of punctuation is consistent with Crane's tendency to increase punctuation
during this period. It is interesting, and possibly
significant, that when the other four texts are ranked in

order of the relative proportion of the spellings 'o' and 'oh', for which Crane's spelling may have changed, the order is the same as that suggested by the punctuation. The order which seems most satisfying, as much on subjective as objective grounds, is MM, TGV, Wiv., Tmp. and WT, but much more work will have to be undertaken on this question for this conclusion to be acceptable generally.

The signs and quality of Crane's influence in the five comedies have been demonstrated and it is not necessary to write more about it by way of conclusion. He was a sophisticating scribe, with strong opinions about what kind of orthography was desirable in texts of this period. He took pride in his manuscription and conceived it as his foremost task to deliver a legible, intelligible manuscript to his client or patron. His obligation was not to the author or to concepts of scholarly accuracy which are held at the present. There is little hope, although his influence on orthography is clear enough, that all the points at which he altered the substantives of his copy texts have been detected by modern scholars and much of his influence will continue to elude detection. There is some reason for confidence in his intelligence and accuracy in reproducing the text where it did not challenge his zeal for orthographical refinement, and, doubtless, when editors come to a greater understanding of his habits, they can make suitable allowance for them.

His influence was so strong that it obscures evidence of the kind of manuscript which he transcribed. I have

commented on this and on the opinions of editors because
it is not possible to allow for Crane's influence without
taking into account the sort of scribal task he had to
undertake. I have found it difficult to explain his
choice of massed entries for three of the five comedies,
and I am reluctant to believe that he adopted this convention from Jonson's example without adequate reason.[150]
Jonson's 1616 Folio must have been influential when
Crane considered the best means to make his transcripts
attractive to patrons and clients and, as has already
been noted, there are indications that some of Jonson's
practices influenced his methods. But had Jonson's
style of setting out scene headings seemed attractive to
Crane, he would, it is reasonable to conjecture, have
used it more often in his transcripts. If he used massed
entries in TGV, why did he not also use them in Tmp.?
A clue to his choice might be found in the status of the
texts which he transcribed. I have rejected Greg's
view that TGV and Wiv. were copied from the prompt-book
and so all five comedies must have been transcribed from
foul papers or, like WT, transcripts of them. Two non-Shakespearian transcripts by Crane with massed entries
were Game Malone (1625) and Q1 Duchess of Malfi (1623).
The first was a greatly abbreviated text of a work of
which he had made at least three previous transcripts;
it is easy to see that the method of preparing massed
entries would have ensured that entries for all the
characters were correctly supplied, and that internal
entries would be unnecessary. The title-page of Webster's
play advertises that it contained 'diuerse things
printed that the length of the Play would not beare in
the Presentment.' Its recent editor was unable to

decide whether Crane had transcribed the prompt-book, where scenes which were not performed might remain as deletions, or the author's papers.[151] However, the quarto was published under the supervision of the author whose dedication it bears. He would not have been human had he not wished to revise his manuscript, and amendments would be found only in his own papers. These might therefore have been so obscure and confused as to commend massed entries to Crane.

Both TGV and Wiv. have signs that the text which was printed in the Folio had been revised, and if the text had been revised, the foul papers were probably 'fouler' than those of Tmp. and MM.[152] Apart from the 'Time' chorus, which some critics have seen as an interpolation by another hand, WT lacks convincing evidence of revision. It may be set apart without harm to the tentative suggestion that disorder in foul papers caused by revision led Crane to mass entrances at the beginning of scenes. The nature of the question does not admit certainty. Nevertheless, it is preferable to seek an explanation of the practice in the character of the papers the scribe had for transcription than to accept unquestioningly that he adopted a quasi-classical literary convention inconsistently from transcript to transcript as he chose.

NOTES
====

References in the Notes to 'Greg' and 'Hinman' are to The Shakespeare First Folio (Oxford, 1955) and The Printing and Proof-Reading of the First Folio of Shakespeare (Oxford, 1963) respectively. Full details of works mentioned by short-title may be consulted in the Bibliography.

---

1. 'Ralph Crane, scrivener to the King's Players', Library ser 4 7: 194-215 S '26.

2. My work on Crane began with a doctoral thesis, 'Spelling analysis and Ralph Crane, a preparatory study of his life, spelling and scribal habits', submitted at Victoria University of Wellington, New Zealand, in 1960. It was examined by the late G. I. Duthie, Regius professor of English at Aberdeen University. The thesis was intended to prepare the way for the work on the Folio which has been undertaken since and which is described here. At that time little was known of how Professor Charlton Hinman was to assign the pages of the First Folio amongst Jaggard's compositors and all students in this field were uncomfortably aware that when his work was published, many conventional views about the printing of the Folio would be upset. I was not willing then to attempt the compositor attributions which would have enabled me to discount the influence of the different Folio compositors on the text when I came to apply my knowledge of Crane's scribal habits to the Folio. This turned out to be a wise decision for even Hinman's laborious and meticulous studies proved unable to distribute all the pages of the Folio with surety amongst the compositors.

The thesis included chapters on the technique and principles of spelling analysis, published with some changes as 'Spelling and the bibliographer', (<u>Library</u> ser 5 18:1-28 Mr '63), and an account of <u>Crane's</u> life and works, and of his scribal practices. The longest section discussed his spellings in the dramatic and poetical works he transcribed between 1618 and 1632. The only topic of Shakespearian interest mentioned was Wilson's views on Crane's relations with the King's Men, and the likelihood of his having been employed to transcribe manuscripts for publication. The discussion of Crane's habits was descriptive rather than analytical and was in general limited to notes on the superficial characteristics of his transcripts. For the present study, the dramatic transcripts have been examined afresh, and I have made little use of my earlier notes here.

More important, however, was an extensive appendix which listed Crane's spellings gathered from his transcripts: this was the list which one hoped would aid examination of the Folio texts which are thought to have been printed from Crane's transcripts. However, although the spelling list has since been expanded, the spellings which have been used for the present investigation have also been gathered afresh. This was necessary for many reasons. The early list drew upon all Crane's transcripts, both dramatic and poetical, but some of his spelling habits changed over the span of years they cover. For instance, for 'fixt/fixd', 'glory/glorie', 'onely/only' and 'vertues/virtues', the first spelling of each pair gave way to the second around 1624-6. Some spellings changed during the years in which he made his dramatic transcripts. 'Break' is the preferred spelling of <u>Pleasure</u>, <u>Barnavelt</u> and <u>Game</u> Folger, 1618-24, but 'breake' is used thenceforth in <u>Game</u> Lansdowne, <u>Game</u> Malone, <u>Witch</u>, <u>Demetrius</u> and in his holograph dedications to 1632. Allowance for such variation was necessary in a list of spellings compiled for use with the Folio, for which any copy Crane transcribed must have been made in the early years of his career as a literary scribe. Further, such was the extent of his surviving dramatic transcripts that samples of only a fifth of the <u>Game</u> transcripts, <u>Witch</u> and <u>Demetrius</u> were drawn on for the spelling list. For <u>Barnavelt</u> I had to depend on Miss Frijlinck's edition, which has so many errors that it is unsuitable for close study of the text. Finally, because my means and facilities were not lavish in 1960, I could not study Crane's homographic spellings and elisions as meticulously as I should have done. The present work has used concordances prepared with the aid of a computer, which are similar in arrangement to the Oxford old-spelling Shakespeare concordances. In addition, more subtle analytical computer programs written to examine Crane's spelling and orthography have allowed me to treat of aspects of his work more authoritatively than I could in the early study. (There is a microfilm copy of my 1960 thesis in Goldsmiths Library, University of London).

3. Ralph Crane, The Works of Mercy, London, 1621. (STC 5986), sig. A6r. The Preface is printed in italic; the underlined words here are in roman type.

4. Greg, p. 100. Nevertheless, the editor of the New Penguin Tempest describes Crane as 'attached to Shakespeare's company as a scrivener.' (p. 179).

5. See Bald, A Game of Chesse, by Thomas Middleton. (1929), pp. 19-25 ('Stage history').

6. Miss Frijlinck, the editor of Barnavelt (1922), pp. xviii-xix, derived these dates from a contemporary reference in the text (lines 1951 and 2020) and a letter from Thomas Locke to Carlton, the English ambassador at the Hague. (P.R.O. Ms. State papers, domestic, v. 110, doc. 18).

7. Dramatic Documents, (1931), p. 269.

8. Wilson, ('Ralph Crane, scrivener to the King's Players', Library ser 4 7:194-215 S '26), p. 212 n., did not agree with Miss Frijlinck that these words were in a different hand.

9. A stage-direction in Game which suggests Crane's interference with copy, is at 5.1.40 where the Trinity and Bridgewater-Huntington transcripts by Middleton give the direction, 'Musique an Altar discouerd and Statues ...'. (The second manuscript was shared with two scribes, but the part to which I refer is in Middleton's hand). This is also the reading of Crane's Folger transcript. In that tran-

script, however, he has added, opposite the line
'and those Brazen Statues moue,' (5.1.48), the
stage-direction 'The Statues moue, & Dance.' This
direction also occurs in his Lansdowne and Malone
transcripts but in those transcripts, 'Statues' has
become 'Images' in both stage-directions.

10. Greg, Dramatic Documents, (1931), p. 273; Shakespeare First Folio, (1955), p. 134.

11. The book-keeper whose hand is seen in Barnavelt has not been identified. None of the dramatic manuscripts of the 1615-25 period which has been published by the Malone Society has any hand resembling that in Barnavelt. It is clearly not that of Edward Knight who, as Greg observed, was named amongst the 'Musitions and other necessary attendantes' of the King's Company in a protection against arrest dated December 27th, 1624. (Greg, pp. 78-9). Greg wrote that it was possible that he was the book-keeper when copy was being prepared for the Folio a few years earlier, but it would be unwise to take this as fact without documentary or textual evidence of Knight's influence in the Folio. Although J. H. P. Pafford in 1963 drew attention to punctuation in some stage-directions in WT which resembled Knight's in his extant prompt-books of later date, I was able to show that his evidence could not bear the weight he put on it. (New Arden The Winter's Tale (1963), p. xix. Rf. 'Knight, Crane, and the copy for the Folio Winter's Tale', N&Q 211:139-40 Ap '66).

12. There is an admirable summary of this controversy in F. P. Wilson's 'Shakespeare and the "New Bibliography"', in The Bibliographical Society, 1892-1942: Studies in Retrospect (1945), pp. 110-11, brought up to date by dame Helen Gardner in a second revised edition, 1970.

13. Greg, p. 100 (Note D).

14. Wilson, 'Shakespeare and the "New Bibliography"', (1945), p. 111.

15. Already mentioned are these plays: 2H4, (M. A. Shaaber, New Variorum ed.) and Tim. (H. J. Oliver, New Arden

ed.). J. M. Nosworthy, Shakespeare's Occasional Plays (1965), p. 230 n., suggests Jn. as another Folio text printed from a Crane transcript.

16. The Bibliography supplies details of the modern editions and discussions of Crane's transcripts, which are described also in my 'Spelling Analysis and Ralph Crane' (1960), chapter [5], 'Crane's works'. His transcripts of Sir Henry Mainwaring's Seaman's Glossary and his holographic Rejoinder to a Bill of Complaint have been discovered recently; they were unknown to Wilson and Greg. I have not made much use of them here since they were written after 1625, but they are described briefly in the Bibliography.

17. Massed entries are discussed on pp. 19-21.

18. Jonson's Masque of Queens is printed and discussed in Herford and Simpson, Ben Jonson, v. 7 (1941), pp. [265]-317.

19. Game Folger, 2.1.355: '"the Eare of State is quick and iealious.' on p. 21 of the transcript. See pp. 136-7 for a discussion of The Duchess of Malfi.

20. The watermarks are identified and their appearance in Witch, Game Malone, and Demetrius (which is dated 27 November, 1625) is discussed by Greg and F. P. Wilson in their Malone Society reprint of Witch (1950), p. viii.

21. Hinman, v. 1, p. 363-4. This date could be a month or more either way (p. 364), but my argument is not affected by any such small variation.

22. Greg, p. 418. The influence of Tmp. on the following Folio comedies is discussed on pp. 107-8.

23. Miss Frijlinck's edition of Barnavelt aimed at reproducing the original 'with strict fidelity on the principles followed in the publications of the Malone Society' (p. xii). She also acknowledged the assistance of Sir Walter Greg, who at that time was the Malone Society's general editor, 'for his unceasing kindness in checking the proofsheets with

the manuscript' (Preface, p. [2]). This is hardly
credible, so many are the errors in the text.
Fortunately, most of the errors affect only the
spellings but there are enough of them to make it
hazardous to use her edition for detailed textual
study. I have rectified the edition's mistakes
from the manuscript and a Xerox copy of it.

Two pages of Pleasure are reproduced by
Herford and Simpson, sufficient to show that the
editors were not always successful in distinguishing
Crane's italic from his secretary hand. (Ben Jonson,
v. 7 (1941), pp. 475-91). At that time it was not
known that Crane was the scribe. Because the
manuscript is not available, I have had to rely on
Herford and Simpson's transcript, but for a concordance and analysis of the text it was corrected
where-ever possible from the plates, and manuscript
readings restored which they had relegated to the
footnotes.

I have not been able to see the manuscript of
Demetrius and perforce have relied on the Malone
Society edition which, for concording, I have
brought as far as possible into conformity with my
conventions elsewhere. That the text is accurate
in all important respects is guaranteed by the name
of the general editor, F. P. Wilson, but it would
have been helpful to have had a copy of the
manuscript to compare with copies of other texts
in my possession.

Difficulties which cannot lightly be overcome
arise when works in the same hand are transcribed
by different editors at wide intervals of time,
especially if, sometimes, the identity of the scribe
was not known. Even the authority of Greg does not
encourage the conclusion that there are no
inconsistencies amongst the editions of Crane's
transcripts. Miss Frijlinck for example refused to
admit the form 'yo^W' which seemed quite clear to me.
Closer inspection showed the 'w' to be a 'u' in
which the final ascending stroke was extended in
the fashion of a 'w'; but the curve at the bottom
of the letter, and the absence of such a 'w' in
any other context, show that it was rightly
transcribed as 'u'. However, 'yo^W' is printed in

the Malone Society editions of <u>Witch</u> and <u>Demetrius</u>: whether it is read as 'yo^u' or 'yo^w' depends on the judgement of the editor as to how far Crane extended the tail of the 'u'. Other inconsistencies amongst editions in the interpretation of various initial letters as miniscules or majuscules have obliged me to transcribe the manuscripts independently: my transcripts will not be more correct but should be more consistent in the treatment of forms which are ambiguous in Crane's transcript. However, as has already been noted, the manuscripts of <u>Pleasure</u> and <u>Demetrius</u> were not available for retranscription.

Quotations from the texts discussed here, or general statements about or statistics of the appearance of certain features of the transcripts might appear to be contradicted by the evidence of the published editions. In cases where I am not obviously in error, this arises from my retranscription of Crane's transcripts.

24. This page is also reproduced in the Malone Society edition.

25. The significance of such variation for the Folio is discussed on pp. 75-8.

26. I cite this example only because the plate can be seen in the Malone Society edition.

27. Herford and Simpson, <u>Ben Jonson</u>, v. 9 (1950), p. 46.

28. The extensive literature on massed entrances and assembling is surveyed by F. P. Wilson in 'Shakespeare and the "New Bibliography"' (1945), pp. 110-12. The massed entrances of the Folio comedies are discussed in chapter 5.

29. Bald, <u>A Game at Chesse, by Thomas Middleton</u>, (1929), p. 42.

30. 'Seuerally' occurs in stage-directions in <u>Barnavelt</u>, 5.3, <u>Game</u> Malone and Folger, 2.2, <u>Game</u> Lansdowne, 2.2.91, and in <u>Demetrius</u> in 'Exeunt seuerally' at 1.566. Its use in the massed entry for act 3 of <u>Game</u> Malone confirms it as Crane's, for Middleton's <u>Game</u> Trinity has only 'Enter ... both the houses'.

31. These transcriptions ignore preliminary dashes, and words like 'A | Domb | Showe' (Malone, 4.3) supplied in braces on the side.

32. Bald, <u>Bibliographical Studies in the Beaumont & Fletcher Folio</u>, (1938), pp. 76-7.

33. Greg, p. 172 (Note P); he supplies a list of 'missing' directions. Directions in <u>Game</u> Folger not in the <u>Trinity</u> transcript occur at <u>Ind</u>. 83, 1.1.75, 262, 360, 2.1.226, 3.1.186, 317, 4.4.79 and 4.4.117. The first is also in Lansdowne, Malone and Q3, the next two in <u>Game</u> Lansdowne.

34. Greg, <u>The Witch</u> (Malone Society, 1950), p. xii.

35. Wilson and Cook, <u>Demetrius</u> (Malone Society, 1951), p. viii.

36. Wilson, <u>Winter's Tale</u> (New Cambridge edition, 1959), p. 118.

37. Other stage-directions tending to support the view that they were written in after the main dialogue are, in <u>Barnavelt</u>, 'Enter Holderus' on f. 10. Since the scribe reserved the last of four columns of the page for the directions, it is not likely that there would be many examples of accommodation of stage-directions to the text. There was also ample room for long lines and the insertion of marginal stage-directions. In <u>Witch</u>, at l. 17, 'Enter Almachildes' is written above the first line on the page, below the ruling. At l. 19 'she Coniures' commences a four line direction which starts above the line to which it refers and is cramped to avoid a long line of text beneath it. At l. 30 there is a three line direction which starts above the line so it could be fitted in. At l. 39 'Enter Francisca' is placed seven lines before the speech-prefix '<u>Fra</u>.' and 'Francisca' is cramped by a long line of text which itself shows no signs of contraction. At l. 42, 'Enter Gaspero' is erased and written in correctly later in the text. At l. 61, 'Enter Duchess' is written above the first line of the text. However, the 'Ex^t.'s, etc., in Crane's current italic hand, are written 'on the line', with preliminary dashes which are also

properly aligned.

In <u>Game</u> Folger on p. 45 a direction commencing 'Enter Bl. B^p.' is written so as to avoid a long line beneath.

In <u>Game</u> Lansdowne on p. 29 a three line direction is crowded into the top right-hand corner, above the first line of text. On p. 51 there is a three line direction written between two long lines of text, and on p. 66 there is a two line direction written above a long line which starts <u>above</u> a previous exit.

In <u>Demetrius</u> the Malone Society editor noted on p. 111 that the 'Exit' in l. 2946 prevented the lower limb of the bracket in a marginal direction being extended to include the last word of the direction.

38. Greg points out a passage in <u>Sir Thomas More</u> (Addition VI, hand B) which was marked for omission. 'The absence ... of speakers' names ... shows that this scribe at least wrote his text first and inserted his speakers afterwards ...', (<u>The Book of Sir Thomas More</u>, Malone Society, 1911), p. 91.

39. McKerrow, 'A suggestion regarding Shakespeare's manuscripts' (<u>RES</u> 11:459-65 Oc '35), p. 464.

40. 'Ralph Crane's parentheses', <u>N&Q</u> 210:334-40 S '65.

41. <u>Op. cit.</u>, pp. 339-40. The discussion there of the parentheses in the Folio cannot be now accepted as new compositor identifications have altered the counts from which the compositors' habits were assessed.

42. J. Leeds Barroll, <u>Shakespeare Studies</u> 2:39 '66.

43. Partridge, <u>Orthography in Shakespeare</u>, (1964), p. 173.

44. A. H. Bullen, ed. <u>Middleton's Works</u>, (1885), v. 5.

45. Brown, The Duchess of Malfi (Revels plays, 1964), pp. lxv-lxvi.

46. J. W. Harper, the most recent editor of Game (New Mermaid series, 1966), accepts most of the stops in Game Folger and retains many of the commas Crane altered to colons.

47. See however the discussion of elisions on pp. 43-5.

48. Greg 'Some notes on Crane's manuscript of The Witch', Library ser 4 22:208-22 Mr '42.

49. In many of these compounds, but not 'pree-thee, the hyphen serves to indicate that metrical stress is to be given to the first part of the compound.

50. Jonson's account of 'Apostrophus' in his English Grammar, with examples from early writings, may be consulted in Herford and Simpson, Ben Jonson, v. 8, (1947), p. 528.

51. Herford and Simpson, Ben Jonson, v. 9, (1950), p. 50 describe the Jonsonian elision as 'the use of an apostrophe between two unelided but lightly sounded syllables to indicate that they are metrically equivalent to one syllable.'

52. There are two 'ile's in Pleasure.

53. The small number of Jonsonian elisions in Demetrius (14) supports my conjecture from the evidence of parentheses (see p. 35) that Crane transcribed Demetrius from an earlier copy in his hand. If this is correct, then Demetrius, like Game Malone, should show lines in which faulty metre could be corrected by restoring apostrophes in Jonsonian elisions which Crane had substituted for the elisions in Fletcher's manuscript. One such line is 1303 where, according to the Malone Society editors, the metre requires 'ye'haue' for 'ye haue'.

54. McKerrow, Prolegomena (1939, repr. 1969), p. 24.

55. See Kökeritz, Shakespeare's Pronunciation (1953), p. 30.

56. See Kökeritz, ib., p. 324.

57. Nosworthy, 'The Songs in The Witch and Ralph Crane' in Shakespeare's Occasional Plays (1965), p. 230.

58. Herford and Simpson, Ben Jonson, v. 7, (1941), p. 477.

59. At l. 2742 in Demetrius, 'Attendants' for 'attendance' is of this kind. Note also 'Silence' for 'Silens' at Witch, l. 298. (See also note 118).

60. Nosworthy, op. cit., p. 231.

61. This spelling list may be consulted in my 1960 thesis.

62. Greg, Shakespeare First Folio, (1955); see especially Tmp., and TGV, pp. 217-18.

63. I assume for the moment that Greg was right to believe that Crane prepared the copy for the five comedies,

64. Hinman, v. 1, p. 363, places the printing of Tmp., TGV and Wiv. in February-March, 1622.

65. See pp. 135-8.

66. Other than those not hitherto associated with him; Hinman, v. 2, p. 521.

67. Greg, p. 417, commented that the transcript of WT with its massed entrances, 'even if the printer returned it, would have been of no use on the stage'.

68. Once this question has been decided, his influence on substantives becomes the most important matter to be examined.

69. F. Kermode, ed. The Tempest (6th Arden ed., repr. 1962), p. xcii, cites this scene heading as evidence that the first page of Tmp. was the first of the Folio to be printed.

70. This has been discussed on p. 18.

71. See for instance, 'Exeunt omn.' set in roman type on Y1^v of AWW after the epilogue which was in italic.

72. These may be seen on Tmp. A5, B2, 2^v, 4; TGV B4^v, C2-3, D1^v; Wiv. D2, 4, 5; and WT Aa5^v, 6.

73. Hinman, v. 1, p. 38.

74. Greg, p. 418. The 'Names of the Actors' is printed next to the epilogue for Tmp. on B4. I cannot see how the function of this list is different from the others. The list in WT, according to the New Arden editor (p. 2) 'was probably drawn up and put in at the printing house ...'.

75. Indented multi-line stage-directions occur occasionally in pages set by the other compositors who arranged directions with a longer but not full-width line followed by increasingly-shorter lines centered beneath the first. The influence of copy is not suggested.

76. Greg, p. 355, observed that the list for MM omits the justice and Varrius, and gives 'Clowne' for Pompey. There is a more detailed discussion in the New Arden edition, p. xxv.

77. Massed entrances are also discussed on pp. 139-40.

78. A more elaborate statistical analysis than the simple proportions provided here would reveal how the compositors' habits varied, but as the table suggests that the copy was more influential on the frequency of the punctuation than compositorial variability, I have chosen to limit the figures to the easily comprehended proportions.

79. Or, of course, a number of sources with similar orthographical characteristics.

80. See p. 32.

81. See pp. 135-8.

82. It will be recalled that the counts of capitals exclude capitals beginning lines of verse, even

though the first word might be a proper noun, and capitals in speech-prefixes and acronyms, and following full stops, exclamation and interrogation marks.

83. There are no colons, exclamation or interrogation marks in Shakespeare's share of Addition II of STM.

84. Greg, pp. 418, 217, 335, 356, 415.

85. There are no parentheses in Shakespeare's share of Addition II of STM.

86. See pp. 34-5.

87. The words were 'Angelo, Anne, Ariel/l, Broome, Camillo, Claudio, Ford, Hermione, Iohn, Isabell/a, Iulia, Lady, Leontes, Lord, Lucetta, Madam/e, Miranda, Page, Paulina, Perdita, Pompey, Protheus, Siluia, sirha/sirrah, Stephano, Thurio, Trinculo' and 'Valentine'.

88. This, and the kind of elisions in AWW, make a transcript more likely as copy.

89. Addition II of STM, in Shakespeare's hand, supplies significant evidence of Shakespeare's habits, but the texts of good authority require detailed examination before the extent of the influence of copy on Crane, and how far he transmitted the author's spelling and contractions, can be discussed.

90. Although 'thart' occurs in Addition II of STM, it is not to be found in any good quarto, according to Partridge (Orthography in Shakespeare 1964, p. 63).

91. See p. 51.

92. Howard-Hill, 'Spelling and the bibliographer', (1963), discusses the use of spellings as evidence in textual inquiries at some length.

93. See note 99.

94. W. S. Kable, 'Compositor B, the Pavier quartos, and copy spellings', Studies in Bibliography 21:131-61 '68.

95. Kable, ib., pp. 157-9.

96. Sometimes, of course, the compositor's inconsistency may produce anomalous spellings.

97. This is particularly true of the most frequently-occurring and common spellings like 'which, your, him, at' and 'on' for which variant spellings were rare in printed works in this period.

98. The assumption here and elsewhere is that Crane's spellings in the hypothecated copy would be his usual or 'preferred' spellings.

99. Tables of variant spellings in the five early comedies may be consulted at pp. 152-4 (Appendix 7). Crane himself did not use '-ie' or '-y' consistently.

100. If MM was Crane's first experience of transcribing Shakespeare's foul papers, these might be his copy spellings.

101. I was informed, after these tests were made, by Mr. P. W. M. Blayney that his independent investigation of the spellings of the Pavier quartos cast some doubt on Dr. Kables figures and calculations, and on the conclusions which could be drawn from them.

102. J. W. Lever, ed. Measure for Measure, (New Arden ed., 1965), p. xii.

103. Words ending in '-nes' in the five comedies which were evidently Crane's habitual spellings are 'basenes, busines, goodnes, greatnes, highnes, kindnes, strangenes, sweetnes, wantonnes, whitenes' and 'witnes'. Other spellings for which Crane's habit is not indicated by the dramatic transcripts are 'closenes, doublenes, fewnes, likenes' and 'newnes'.

104. Julius Caesar, (New Cambridge ed., 1949), p. 93.

105. Other plays of Shakespeare's last period, e.g. H8 and Cym. have many more such apostrophes,

occasioned by the development of his language.

106. 1.1.64 n.

107. The New Arden collation (2.1.273) does not record the apostrophe.

108. See pp. 39-42.

109. Greg, *Editorial Problems*, (2d ed., 1951), p. 152; New Arden *Tempest*, (6th ed., 1958; repr. 1962), p. xii.

110. Mentioned by Greg, p. 415, n. 3

111. New Arden *Tempest*, p. xi.

112. Greg, p. 420.

113. The recorded performance of *Tmp*. nearest the publication of the Folio was at court during the winter of 1612-13 (New Arden *Tempest*, p. xxii). It is hard to believe that Crane would have retained clear memories of the masque elements of the action to 1619 before which it is unlikely he would have made the transcript.

114. New Arden *Tempest*, pp. 161-5.

115. The tables of readings which are supplied for the five comedies are not given to show the amount of emendation that is wanted, for there are many places where errors are suspected but emendation has not been made. The tables show, however, the kinds of error which modern editors have found in these comedies. The New Arden editions were chosen for the convenience of their collations.

116. New Arden *Tempest*, p. xci.

117. The third form illustrated by McKerrow, *Introduction to Bibliography* (1927), fig. 22, p. 343.

118. New Arden *Tempest*, p. 169. The same error occurs in *Ed3* on B4, line 364: 'Being in the sacred present of a King'.

119. See pp. 132-3.

120. This is a Middleton spelling in Game. Crane's own spelling, when he did not use the Jonsonian form, was probably 'shee'ld', by analogy with similar elisions in his dramatic transcripts.

121. Clifford Leech, ed. The Two Gentlemen of Verona (New Arden ed., 1969), pp. xiii-xv, supplies the best recent discussion of massed entrances.

122. Greg, pp. 217-18.

123. See pp. 139-40.

124. The New Arden edition does not print or record it (4.1.3).

125. Entries supplied in place of massed entries and other directions like 'aside's are not listed in the tables of readings. They also take no account of mislining, incorrect verse and prose, punctuation, and manifest compositorial misprints (turned letters and the like).

126. W. G. Clark and J. Glover, ed. The Works of William Shakespeare (Cambridge, 1863), v. 1, p. 254.

127. Greg, (Shakespeare's Merry Wives of Windsor, 1602. Oxford, 1910, p. xiii) also thought that the fifth act may have been worked over by another hand.

128. Greg, p. 337.

129. See pp. 139-40. H. J. Oliver, the New Arden editor, does not discuss the provenance of Crane's copy.

130. Readings at 1522, 1635 and 2382 are probably misprints, whereas the New Arden readings at 1364, 2306, 2307 and 2421 are modernisations.

131. New Arden Measure for Measure (1965), p. xxxi.

132. See Howard-Hill, 'The compositors of the Folio comedies', SB (1973), XXV.

133. See pp. 139-40.

134. New Arden Measure for Measure, p. xxv.

135. The nine interior entries set alongside the dialogue at the right of the column in Tmp. by compositors A(F) and C give further evidence that their copy was a Crane transcript. Compositor B, with only one exception (WT Bb2^v:2005) centered all the interior entrances, as did A(F), C and D in MM, but the compositor A of WT, who may have been unused to setting copy of this kind, set three of the eight interior entrances in his share of the text at the right of the column.

136. Greg, p. 354.

137. Pafford, 'The Winter's Tale: typographical peculiarities in the Folio text' N&Q 206:172-8 My '61.

138. Herford and Simpson, Ben Jonson, v. 10 (1950), p. 590, comment on 'some-it' and 'ouercome-it' in Pleasure and similar uses of hyphens in Tmp. and TGV.

139. If Crane had observed this convention in TGV and Wiv. which also have massed entries, this might be further evidence of the separate identities of compositor A of the early comedies and A of WT and the histories. Colons mark off entries in Game Malone: see 'Enter Ignatius: and Error' (f. 3) and the massed entrances for 1.1, 2.1, 3.1, 4.1, 4.2, 4.4, 5.1, 5.2 and 5.3. Characters who enter later are often introduced by 'Then...' in the massed entry.

140. 'Knight, Crane and the copy for the Folio Winter's Tale' N&Q 211:139-40 Ap '66. The preparation of a new prompt-book suggests that the foul papers were not in suitable condition for use in performance.

141. New Arden The Winter's Tale, (1963), pp. xix-xx.

142. Bald, Bibliographical Studies in the Beaumont & Fletcher Folio of 1647, (1938), p. 72.

143. Greg, p. 152. Sir E. K. Chambers (William Shakespeare, 1930, v. 1, pp. 237-42) and Greg, pp. 149-52, discuss the significance of oaths in manuscripts and printed texts.

144. 'a plaigue on them' (176), 'byth mas' (181), 'before god' (211), 'marry god' (219) and 'faith' (264).

145. Chambers, op. cit., p. 240. He points out that 'we cannot tell how much profanity the reporters may have contributed.'

146. Walker, Textual Problems of the First Folio, (1953), p. 31. 'Broadly, the dividing line between plays from which profanity was not expurgated and those from which it was lies between the Comedies and the Histories' ('Quarto 'copy' and the 1623 Folio: 2 Henry IV', Review of English Studies new series 2:217-25 Jl '51, p. 225).

147. Some hyphens which are probably compositorial are those which McKerrow (Introduction to Bibliography, p. 314) discusses. They were used to separate combinations of long 's' and other characters, particularly 'm', and 'f' or 's' when the appropriate ligature was not available, which the compositors thought were typographically unattractive. There are many instances in Duchess of Malfi (1623) in which the long 's' is kerned and also in the Folio, where, although the 's' does not appear to be kerned, the compositors sometimes set hyphens as if it was.

148. There is a detailed examination of the first quarto of Duchess of Malfi in J. R. Brown, 'The printing of John Webster's plays', Studies in Bibliography 6:117-40 '54; 8:113-27 '56; 15:57-69 '62. Other good evidence of Crane is the spelling 'ceize' on L1 (see also p. 144) and spellings like 'sadnes' ending in 'nes'.

149. This was discussed on pp. 32-33.

150. The general question was mentioned on pp. 20-1 and 79-80.

151. J. R. Brown, ed. *The Duchess of Malfi*, (Revels plays 1964, pp. lxvi-lxviii.

152. See pp. 113 and pp. 118-19.

APPENDICES

APPENDIX 1: VARIANT READINGS IN GAME LANSDOWNE AND MALONE

This table shows the variant readings of Game Lansdowne and Malone, excluding stage-directions and elision variants. A reading which is substantially that of the Trinity transcript has been identified with an asterisk.

Bald's act/ sc. no.	Lansdowne	Malone
1.1.25*	the Enemie	your Enemie:
1.1.69	Entrances	*Entrance,
1.1.81	no	*not
1.1.180	Which	*that
1.1.238*	Virgin)	Lady)
1.1.249*	would	will
1.1.289*	publique)	privat)
1.1.292*	keepe	be
2.1.117*	'blesse me: 'threatens	... he threatens
2.1.137	thy Loue,	*my Loue,
2.1.154*	resist me.	resist.
2.1.155*	help: oh help:	help: help: oh help.
2.1.167*	I will	And will
2.1.205*	I haue don't then:	Be it thus then.
2.2.18*	---	Goe, be gon:
2.2.35*	I haue	But I haue
2.2.96*	I play	And play
3.1.46-7*	through the submissiue acknowledgement of your disobedience	(through your submissiue acknowledgement)
3.1.215*	fowle Attemptor	falce-Attemptor
3.1.357*	You know me:	You know me well enough:
3.3.60	yours:	*yours: How doe you?

APPENDICES 161

Bald's act/ sc. no.	Lansdowne	Malone
4.1.126	wh.Qs.P.	*Bl.Qs.P.
4.1.172*	work'd	wrought
4.2.15*	I, you	you
4.2.59*	'pray	I'pray
4.2.73*	powre	Powres
4.2.74*	Side	State,
4.2.92	poundes	*Pound,
4.2.94	Killing, &c.	Killing
4.2.120	true: that	*True (Sir) that
4.2.126	at Antwerpe.	*of Antwerpe.
4.4.17	what paine	*what a paine
4.4.65*	downe.	downe: there is no remedie.
4.4.80*	lives	live
4.4.87*	wh.Q.	wh.Qs.
4.4.98*	well with	well indeed with
5.2.122*	wh.Q.	wh.Qs.P.
5.3.120	our Faithes, or Praires,	*our Faithes: our Praiers,
5.3.201	heads	*Fore-heads

APPENDIX 2: CONJECTURAL EMENDATIONS IN THE WITCH

This list of the conjectural emendations in Witch in the editions of Reed (R), Dyce (D), and Bullen (B) has been compiled from the collation of the Malone Society reprint (M).

Line No.	Crane's transcript	Correction	Editor
46	King's	Duke's	D
73	knew	know	D
149	Fate-on't	Face on't	R
187	Hellwin, & Prickle	Hellwain, & Puckle	D
205	or	o'er	M
217	wlelplies	Whelplies	R
227	back	black	R
298	Silence	Silens	M

162 CRANE AND SOME FOLIO COMEDIES

Line No.	Crane's transcript	Correction	Editor
308	they're wretched things	they're th'wretched'st things	M
320	and	as	D
411	Stalamprey	Sealamprey	D
471	Ponado	Panado	D
603-4	---	Enter Aberzanes, with Servants.	Ancient British Drama, 1810.
610	---	Exeunt Servants	D
857	rude	rulde	Ancient British Drama, 1810.
882	---	Exit Woman	M
886	fashion:	fashion	M
934	---	Enter Boy.	M
1038	Citty-tuck	Citty-truck	B
1141	five	fine	M
1203	---	Exit Francisca.	Ancient British Drama, 1810.
1300	---	Exeunt all the Witches except Hecate.	D
1364	our Mistris Fountaines	Over misty Hills and Fountains	1673 Mac.
		Over Hills, and misty Fountains	1674 D'Avenant
1365	Steepe	Steeples	1673 Mac.
1435	Enter | L. Gouerno^r	Enter Lord Gouernor, attended by Gentlemen.	D
1438	---	Exeunt Gentlemen.	D
1496	Man	Men	D
1546	---	Exit Florida.	M
1553	feele	feede (fill?)	M
1560	---	Exit Sebastian.	M
1669	---	Exit Gaspero.	M
1680	Fra.	Flo. [within]	D
1713	Ruynes	Ruynous	D
1750	---	Exit Francisca above.	D
1767	Sebastian	Antonio	R

Line No.	Crane's transcript	Correction	Editor
1768	Seb.	An.	R
1771	Seb.	An.	R
1800	---	Enter Francisca.	M
1817	---	Enter Hermio.	M
1827	---	Exeunt Aberzanes and Francisca.	M
1849	fo't	for't	M
1900	---	Exit Florida and Gaspero.	M
1901	yf	Gou. yf	R
1928	3ª	2ª	R
1982	---	Exit Duchess.	M
2003	Liand	Liard	M
2009	againe	a graine	1674 D'Avenant
2014	all Round	All. Round	R
2025	4ª	3ª	R
2050	---	Enter Hermio.	M
2056	how?	who?	D conj.
2079	---	Servants remove Florida.	D
2097	Vrbin	? in error for Ravenna.	M
2118	don	done't	D
2128	thee	there	Ancient British Drama, 1810.
2138	performes	performe	R

APPENDIX 3: VARIANTS IN DEMETRIUS AND THE HUMOUROUS LIEUTENANT, 1647

The following variants in Demetrius and The Humourous Lieutenant, which have been taken from the collation of the Malone Society reprint edited by Margaret McL. Cook and F. P. Wilson (1951), do not include stage-directions and minor variations of punctuation.

Malone Line No.	Demetrius	Humourous Lieutenant
386	some	and some
404	Leo.	Gent.
405-6	---	Lie. (i.e. Leo.)
414	fightes	sighes
672	(sure	'Death
691	see	saw
709	designes	descries
748	Dem.	Leo.
833	send	send (Dyce, following Mason, vend)
1034	pure	poore
1064-5	all ... Dem. that...	Dem. all... that ...
1119	company	competency
1171	promise	promises
1218	be	lie
1291	his angry will, if ere he come to know this,	His anger will inflict, if'ere he know this,
1292	as he shall;	As know he shall
1331-4		1331, 1333, 1332, 1334
1438	help	help't
1464	Gaole	Jade
1584-5		There's ... | There's ... | Or ...
1597	Gentlemen	Gentlewoman
1598	sure	Since
1680	Watches	martches
1742	Dem.	Phis.
1743	Phis.	Dem.
1744	---	Phis.
1854	Dem.	Leo.
1872	Mans	man
1874	price	peace
1932	Exe^t	I'le send a post away.
1958	see	knew
2283	there	then (F2 and Dyce)
2522	wrings	roares
2544	passe	poaze
2561	Footeman	footmen
2567	thou	though
2656	you	you can
2662	sitts vpon our	sitting on your
2718	(Gent?)	---

APPENDICES   165

Malone Line No.	Demetrius	Humourous Lieutenant
2742	Attendants	attendance
2748	vow	way
2767	Gent.	Men.
2901	waies	wiles
2998	and	arm'd
3184	drop'd	crept
3232	once	one
3255	Peace	price
3303	Antiochus	Antigonus

APPENDIX 4: VARIANTS OF COMPOSITOR B'S SPELLINGS IN
            TWELFTH NIGHT

B's spelling	Other spellings*	Crane's spelling
acte	act	act
aid	ayde	aid/e
answer	answere	answere/answeare
approch	approach	approach
authority	authoritie	authoritie
beauty	beautie	beutie
behinde	behind	behind
bloody	bloudie	bloody
	bloudy	
breefe	briefe	breif
cleere	cleare	cleere
company	companie	company
cosin	cosine	cosen
country	countrey	cuntrie/y
	countreyman	
credite	credit	creadit
cruelty	crueltie	crueltie

*A blank in this column signifies that B almost invariably
reproduced the spelling of his copy; the spelling of the
text is listed in the first column. Variant spellings
which apparently were formed by justification have not
been listed.

B's spelling	Other spellings	Crane's spelling
deny	denie	deny
diuell	deuill	deuill
early	earely	early
enemy	enemie	enemy
entreate	entreat	entreate
fancy	fancie	fancy
foorth	forth	forth
happy	happie	happie
heart	hart	hart
houre	howre	howre
ieast	iest	iest
lady	ladie	lady
mad	madde	mad
marry	marrie	marry/mary
master/s	maisters	master/s
month/e/s	moneth/s	moneth/s
necessity	necessitie	necessitie
olde	old	old
pitty	pittie	pittie/y
pretty	prettie	pretty
quickely	quickly	quickly
ready	readie	ready
sunne	sun	sun
together	togither	togeather
truely	truly	truely/truly
twenty	twentie	twentie/y
very	verie	very
wee'l	we'll	wee'll
willingly	willinglie	willingly
yeare/s	yeeres	yeare/yeere/s
yong	young	yong
you'l	you'le	you'll

APPENDIX 5: VARIANTS OF COMPOSITOR B'S SPELLINGS IN ERR.

B's spelling	Other spellings	Crane's spelling
aboard	aboord	Not known
aid	aide	aid/e

B's spelling	Other spellings	Crane's spelling
beauty	beautie	beutie
city	citie	cittie
company	companie	company
credite	credit	creadit
deny	denie	deny
duty	dutie	dutie
euery	euerie	euery
fly	flie	fly
foorth	forth	forth
forty	fortie	forty
fury	furie	fury
greefe	griefe	greif
guilty	guiltie	guilty
heauy	heauie	heauy
high	hie	high
holy	holie	holy/holly
honesty	honestie	honestie
lady	ladie	lady
liberty	libertie	libertie
merry	merrie	merry
misery	miserie	miserie
money	monie	money
	mony	
murther	murder	murder
natiuity	natiuitie	Not known
oh		oh/O
olde	old	old
poyson/s	poisons	poyson/s
run	runne	run
sorry	sorrie	sorry
thirty	thirtie	thirtie
twenty	twentie	twentie/y
vnhappy	vnhappie	happie
war	warre	warr

APPENDIX 6: VARIANTS OF COMPOSITOR B'S SPELLINGS IN SHR.

B's spelling	Other spellings	Crane's spelling
beauty	beautie	beutie

B's spelling	Other spellings	Crane's spelling
body	bodie	body
breefe	briefe	brief
carry	carrie	carry
charity	charitie	charitie
city	citie	cittie
	cittie	
company	companie	company
country	countreyman	cuntrie/y
courtesie		curtesie
courtsie		
curtesie		
credite	credit	creadit
deny	denie	deny
diuell/s	deuils	deuill/s
dowry	dowrie	Not known
duty	dutie	dutie
enuy	enuie	enuy
euery	euerie	euery
extreme/s	extreames	extreame/s
fancy	fancie	fancie
foorth	forth	forth
fury	furie	fury
gyrle	girle	girle
happy	vn/happie	happie
heart/s	harts	harts
heauy	heauie	heauy
hony	honie	honey
ieast	iest/ed	iest/ed
entreate	intreat	entreat
	intreate	
lady	ladie	lady
liberty	libertie	libertie
loud		loud
lowd		lowd
madam	madame	madam
marry	marrie	marry/mary
mercy	mercie	mercie
merry	merrie	merry
mighty	mightie	mightie
money	monie	money
o		o ⎫
oh		oh ⎭
olde	old	old
ready	readie	ready

B's spelling	Other spelling	Crane's spelling
sodaine		sodaine
sorry	sorrie	sorry
sunne	sun	sun
tarry	tarrie	tarry
try	trie	try
twenty	twentie	twentie/y
very	verie	very
wee'l	wee'le	wee'll
	we'l	
yeare/s	yeere/s	yeare/yeere/s
yong		yong
yonger		yonger
yongest		yongest

APPENDIX 7: VARIANTS OF COMPOSITOR B'S SPELLINGS IN Tmp., Wiv., MM AND WT

B's spelling	Frequ.	Other spellings	Frequ.	Crane's spellings

TEMPEST:

B's spelling	Frequ.	Other spellings	Frequ.	Crane's spellings
aboard		aboord	1j	Not known
acte		act	1	act
beauty		beautie	1	beutie
credite		credit	1	creadit
deny		denie	1	deny
euery	4	euerie	1	euery
		eu'ry	1	
fly		flie	1	fly
foorth		forth	4:1	forth
iest/ing		iesting	1	iesting
lowder			1j	lowder
marry	1	marrie	1	marry
noise	1j	noyse/s	2:1	noyce
o	14:3			o ⎫
oh	3			oh ⎭
olde		old	2	old
pitty	1	pity	1	pitty/ie

B's spelling	Frequ.	Other spellings	Frequ.	Crane's spellings

TEMPEST cont.

B's spelling	Frequ.	Other spellings	Frequ.	Crane's spellings
prethee	2:1	pre-thee	3:1	pre-thee
sonne/s	4	son	1	son
sunne		sun	2	sun
twenty		twentie	1	twentie
very	4	verie	1	verie

MERRY WIVES:

B's spelling	Frequ.	Other spellings	Frequ.	Crane's spellings
acte	1	act	1	act
alwayes	1	alwaies	1j	alwaies
blood/y	2	bloud/y	1	blood/y
choise		choice	1	choice
country		countrie	1	cuntrie
diuell	2:4	deuill	1:2	deuill
fly		flye	1:1	fly
foorth		forth	2:3	forth
gyrle		girle	1j	girle
(heartlings)		hartlings	1	hartlings
heartily	1j	hartly	1	hartly
hereticke		heretike	1	heretique
ieast/s		iest/s	3:3	iest/s
many	3	manie	1	many
money	2:3	mony	1	money
o	7:5			o ⎫
oh	4:2			oh ⎭
olde	3j	old	8:5	old
quicke	3j	quick	1	quick
shee'l		she'll	1	shee'll
sodaine	1:1			sodaine
they'l		they'll	1:1	they'll
truely	1j	truly	1:1	truly
wee'l	1:2	wee'll	1:1	wee'll
		we'll	2:2	
yeare/s	1	yeere/s	1	yeare/yeere/s

MEASURE FOR MEASURE:

B's spelling	Frequ.	Other spellings	Frequ.	Crane's spellings
any	3j	anie	1:3	any
answer	2	answere	1:1	answere/answeare

APPENDICES 171

B's spelling	Frequ.	Other spellings	Frequ.	Crane's spellings
MEASURE FOR MEASURE cont.				
bloody		bloudie	1	bloody
body		bodie	3	body
company		companie	1	company
contrary	1j	contrarie	1	Not known
deere	2:1	deare	1	deere
deerely		dearely	1	deerely
euery		euerie	1:2	euery
foorth		forth	1:1	forth
happy		happie	1	happie
heauy		heauie	1	heauy
holy	1	holie	2	holy/holly
ieast		iest	1	iest
many	1j	manie	2:2	many
mercy	1j	mercie	5	mercie
murtherer	1			murderer
noise	2	noyse	1j	noyce
o	2:1			o ⎫
oh	11:3			oh ⎭
olde	1:4	old	3:1	old
onely	1:2	onelie	1	onely
pitty		pitie	1:1	pittie/y
power		powre	1	powre
ready		readie	2:1	ready
twenty		twentie	2	twentie
very	3j	verie	2:3	very
yeare/s	1j	yeere/s	2	yeare/yeere/s
WINTER'S TALE:				
aboard		a-boord	2	Not known
angel		angell	1	angell
answer		answere	1:1	answere/answeare
approch		approach	2:1	approach
briers	1j			Not known
choise		choice	1:1	choice
credite		credit	1	creadit
daily		dayly	1	daylie
deere/st	6:1	deare	1	deere/st
deede/s		deed/s	3:1	deed/es
extreme		extreames	1	extreames/extreemes

B's spelling	Frequ.	Other spellings	Frequ.	Crane's spelling
WINTER'S TALE cont.				
fancy		fancie	1	fancie
foorth		forth	2:1	forth
fury	1	furie	1	fury
gyrle/s		girle/s	1	girle/s
guilty	1	guiltie	1	guiltie/y
happy	1	happie	1	happie
houre	1	howre	1	howre
loud	2			loud/lowd
lowd/er/st	2:1			-ou-/-ow-
mighty		mightie	1:1	mightie
month		moneth	1	moneth
neede	6:2	need	2j	need
o	14:1			o ⎫
oh	8:4			oh ⎭
olde	1:1	old	6:1	old
power/full	1j	powre/s	4	powre/s
run	1	runne	1	run
sonne	8:3	son/-in-law	1:1	son
sunne		sun	4	sun
wee'l	2:3	wee'll	1j	wee'll
yeare/s	2	yeere/s	2:1	yeare/yeere/s
yong	5			yong

BIBLIOGRAPHY

(a) CRANE'S DRAMATIC TRANSCRIPTS

1. [Jonson, Benjamin] Pleasure reconcild to Vertue.
    [1618] (Chatsworth MS.)

    See also nos. 27, 44.

2. [Fletcher, John, and P. Massinger] The Tragedy of
    Sr Iohn Van Olden Barnauelt. [1619] (B.M. MS. Add.
    18653)

    See also nos. 20, 23.

3. Middleton, Thomas. A Song in seuerall parts. 1622.
    (Public Record Office MS. State papers, domestic,
    v. 129, doc. 53)

4. [Middleton, Thomas] A Game att Chesse. 1624.
    (Folger MS. 7043)

    See also nos. 13, 16, 26

5. Middleton, Thomas. A Game at Chesse. [1624]
    (B.M. MS. Lansdowne 690)

    See also no. 13.

6. ----. ----. 1624. (Bodleian Library MS. Malone
    25)

    See also no. 13.

7. ----. A Tragi-Coomodie, called the Witch. [1624-5]
    (Bodleian Library MS. Malone 12)

    See also nos. 24-5, 34.

8. Fletcher, John. <u>Demetrius and Enanthe</u>. [1625]
   (Brogyntyn MS. 42)

   See also nos. 15, 19.

(b) OTHER MANUSCRIPTS MENTIONED

9. Middleton, Thomas. <u>A Game at Chesse</u>. [1624]
   (Trinity College, Cambridge, MS. O.2.66)

   See also no. 13.

10. ----. ----. [1624] (Henry E. Huntington Library MS.)

11. [Crane, Ralph] <u>Rejoinder</u> [1623]

    [The Ioynt and seuerall Answeares of Raph Crane, and Richard Pagett Gent Defend^{te} | to the Bill of Complaint of Richard Crane Gent, Complaynaunt.] (P.R.O. MS. 1623: Requ. 2/393, no. 31)

    This unsigned document was drawn to my attention by Mr. E. A. J. Honigmann on account of its biographical interest. That Crane was the scribe was suggested by a reference to his 'having many | yeeres byn very serviceable to the said Compl^t in Wryting for him...', and the identification was confirmed when it was seen that the Rejoinder, on behalf of two defendants, was in Crane's handwriting. The superscription and endorsement are in another, official, hand.

    The complaint concerns ten pounds which Crane is said to have borrowed about 'six yers sence' (i.e. 1617) towards 'the buying or purchase of a Lease of or in a House', for which he entered into a bond. The document has no other biographical interest, although it is a valuable example of Crane's work-a-day scrivening.

12. Mainwaring, Sir Henry. <u>Seaman's Glossary</u>, 1626.

[A | briefe Abstract, Exposition, and | Demonstration of all | Termes, Parts, and Things | belonging to a Shippe: | And the Practick of | NAVIGATION. | Composed by Sir | Henry Manwayring | knight. | Written by | Raph Crane. | 1626.

4°; p. [1-16] 1-190.

A Xerox copy of this manuscript, which is University of Illinois MS. q387.2 M 28b, was supplied to me on condition that any work making extensive reference to it was to be offered to the University of Illinois Press for publication. The University has not permitted a description of the manuscript to be published. The manuscript was sold at Sotheby's in April, 1964, to Jacob Zeitlin of Los Angeles.

Other transcripts of Mainwaring's work exist in public collections.

(c) PRINTED WORKS ON CRANE OR HIS DRAMATIC TRANSCRIPTS

13. Bald, Robert C., ed. A Game at Chesse, by Thomas Middleton. Cambridge, C.U.P., 1929.

    'The texts' (p. 26-43) includes description and discussion of the Trinity, Huntington, Lansdowne and Malone MSS. 'Characteristics of Crane as a transcriber' (pp. 111-3)

14. ----. A new manuscript of Middleton's Game at Chesse. Mod Lang R 25:474-8 '30.

    The Rosenbach-Folger transcript, not in Crane's hand.

15. ----. Bibliographical Studies in the Beaumont & Fletcher Folio of 1647. [London] Ptd. at the O.U.P. for the Bibliographical Society, 1938. (Bibliographical Society Transactions. Supplement, no. 13)

    'Demetrius and Enanthe' (pp. 64-5)

16. ----. An early version of Middleton's Game at Chesse. Mod Lang R 38:177-80 '43.

    See no. 4.

17. Baldwin, Thomas W. On Act and Scene Division in the Shakspere First Folio. Carbondale, Southern Illinois U.P., 1965.

    Claims that Crane was not responsible for the massed entries but merely the copyist of texts already prepared in this fashion by a 'classical editor'.

18. Brown, John R., ed. The Duchess of Malfi: John Webster. (Revels Plays). London, Methuen [1964]

19. [Cook, Margaret McL. and F. P. Wilson, ed.] Demetrius and Enanthe, by John Fletcher. [London, Ptd. for the Malone Society by C. Batey at the O.U.P.] 1951. (Malone Society Reprints)

    See no. 8.

20. Frijlinck, Wilhelmina P., ed. The Tragedy of Sir John van Olden Barnavelt, anonymous Elizabethan plays. Amsterdam, H. G. van Dorssen; London, H. Milford, O.U.P., 1922.

    'Edition and manuscript' (pp. xi-xv). See no. 2.

21. Graves, Thornton. Ralph Crane and the King's Players. Stud Philol 21:362-6 Ap '24.

22. Greg, Sir Walter W., ed. Shakespeare's Merry Wives of Windsor, 1602. Oxford, Clarendon Press, 1910.

23. ----. Dramatic Documents from the Elizabethan Playhouses. Oxford, Clarendon Press [1931] (Repr. 1969) 2v.

    'Sir John van Olden Barnavelt' (V. 1, pp. 228-9)

24. ----. Some notes on Crane's manuscript of The Witch. Library ser 4 22:208-22 Mr '42.

25. ----. and F. P. Wilson, ed. The Witch, by Thomas Middleton. [London, Ptd. for the Malone Society by C. Batey at the O.U.P.] 1950. (Malone Society Reprints)

26. Harper, J. W., ed. A Game at Chess: Thomas Middleton. (The New Mermaids.) London, E. Benn [1966]

27. Herford, Charles H., P. and Evelyn Simpson, ed. Ben Jonson: volume X: Play commentary, masque commentary. Oxford, 1950. (Repr. [1961]).

   'Pleasure reconciled to virtue' (pp. 573-90)

28. Howard-Hill, Trevor H. Spelling-Analysis and Ralph Crane: a preparatory study of his life, spelling, and scribal habits. Ph.D. thesis, Victoria University of Wellington, New Zealand, 1960.

29. ----. Ralph Crane's parentheses. N&Q 210:334-40 S '65.

30. ----. Knight, Crane and the copy for the Folio Winter's Tale. N&Q 211:139-40 Ap '66.

31. Kermode, J. Frank, ed. The Tempest. (The Arden edition of ... Shakespeare.) [6th ed.] London, Methuen; Cambridge, Mass., Harvard U. P. [1958] (Repr. 1961, 1962)

   'Note additional to Introduction: Ralph Crane and the copy for The Tempest' (pp. lxxxix-xciii)

32. Leech, Clifford, ed. The Two Gentlemen of Verona. (The Arden edition of ... Shakespeare.) London, Methuen [1969]

33. Lever, J. W., ed. Measure for Measure. (The Arden edition of ... Shakespeare.) London, Methuen; Cambridge, Mass., Harvard U.P. [1965]

34. Nosworthy, James M. Shakespeare's Occasional Plays, their Origin and Transmission. London, E. Arnold [1965]

'The songs in The Witch and Ralph Crane' (pp. [227]-31.)

35. Oliver, Harold J., ed. Timon of Athens. (The new Arden edition of ... Shakespeare.) London, Methuen [1959]

36. ----, ed. The Merry Wives of Windsor. (The Arden edition of ... Shakespeare.) London, Methuen [1971]

37. Pafford, John H. P. The Winter's Tale: typographical peculiarities in the Folio text. N&Q 206:172-8 My '61.

38. ----. The Winter's Tale. [4th ed.] (The Arden edition of ... Shakespeare.) London, Methuen; Cambridge, Mass., Harvard U.P. [1963]

39. Partridge, Astley C. Orthography in Shakespeare and Elizabethan Drama; a study of colloquial contractions, elisions, prosody and punctuation. London, E. Arnold [1964]

'The orthographical characteristics of Ralph Crane' (pp. [172]-4)

40. Righter, Anne, ed. William Shakespeare. The Tempest. (New Penguin Shakespeare.) [Harmondsworth, Middlesex] Penguin books [1968]

41. Somer, John L. Ralph Crane and 'an olde play called Winter's Tale'. Emporia State Research Studies 10no4:22-8 '62.

42. Tannenbaum, Samuel A. 'Ralph Crane and The Winter's Tale' in Shaksperian Scraps and other Elizabethan fragments. New York, Columbia U.P., 1933. pp. 75-86.

43. Wilson, Frank P. Ralph Crane, scrivener to the King's Players. Library ser 4 7:194-215 S '26.

44. ----. Ben Jonson and Ralph Crane. TLS 8 N'41.

Identifies Pleasure as being in Crane's hand.

45. Wilson, John D., ed. The Winter's Tale. (New Cambridge edition). Cambridge, C.U.P., 1959. (First ed., 1931)

(d) OTHER PRINTED WORKS MENTIONED AND GENERAL WORKS OF REFERENCE

46. Barroll, J. Leeds. Significant articles, monographs and reviews. Shakespeare Studies 2:34-50 '66.

47. Bentley, Gerald E. The Jacobean and Caroline Stage. Oxford, Clarendon Press [1941-68] 7v.

48. Brown, John R. The printing of John Webster's plays. Studies in Bibliography 6:117-40 '54; 8:113-27 '56; 15:57-69 '62.

49. Bullen, A. H., ed. Middleton's Works. London, 1885. 7v.

50. Chambers, Sir Edmund K. The Elizabethan Stage, Oxford, Clarendon Press [1923] 4v.

51. ----. William Shakespeare, a study of facts and problems. Oxford, Clarendon Press [1930] 2v.

52. Clark, W. G. and J. Glover, ed. The Works of William Shakespeare, Cambridge, 1863.

53. Greg, Sir Walter W., ed. The Book of Sir Thomas More. London [Ptd. for the Malone Society by H. Hart at the O.U.P.] 1911. (Malone Society Reprints)

54. ----. English Literary Autographs, 1550-1650. Oxford, Clarendon Press, 1932.

55. ----. The Editorial Problem in Shakespeare, a survey of the foundations of the text. 2d ed. Oxford, Clarendon Press, 1951. (First ed., 1942; repr. '3d ed.' 1953)

56. ----. The Shakespeare First Folio, its Bibliographical and Textual History. Oxford, Clarendon Press, 1955.

57. Howard-Hill, Trevor H. Spelling and the bibliographer. Library ser 5 18:1-28 Mr '63.

58. ----. The compositors of the Shakespeare Folio comedies. Studies in Bibliography v. 26, 1973.

59. ----, ed. Oxford Shakespeare Concordances. Oxford, Clarendon Press, 1969-72. 37v.

60. Kable, William S. Compositor B, the Pavier quartos, and copy spellings. Studies in Bibliography 21:131-61 '68.

61. Kökeritz, Helge. Shakespeare's Pronunciation. New Haven, Yale U.P.; London, G. Cumberlege, O.U.P., 1953.

62. McKerrow, Ronald B. An Introduction to Bibliography for Literary Students. Oxford, Clarendon Press, 1927. (Repr. 1928...1951)

63. ---. A suggestion regarding Shakespeare's manuscripts. R Eng Stud 11:459-65 Oc '35.

64. ----. Prolegomena for the Oxford Shakespeare, a study in editorial method. Oxford, Clarendon Press, 1939. (Repr. [1969])

65. Shaaber, Matthias A., ed. The second Part of Henry the Fourth. (A new Variorum edition of Shakespeare.) Philadelphia, J. B. Lippincott, 1940.

66. Walker, Alice. Textual Problems of the First Folio... Cambridge, C.U.P., 1953. (Shakespeare Problems series)

67. Wilson, Frank P. 'Shakespeare and the "New Bibliography" in Francis, Sir Frank C., ed. The Bibliographical Society, 1892-1942: Studies in Retrospect. London, Bibliographical Society, 1945. (Repr. 1949; 2d ed., rev. and ed. by dame Helen Gardner. Oxford, Clarendon Press, 1970).

68. Wilson, John D. Julius Caesar. (New Cambridge edition.) Cambridge, C.U.P., 1949.

INDEX

ACT AND SCENE DIVISION   10   19-21
ALCHEMIST, THE   20
ALL'S WELL THAT ENDS WELL
    apostrophes   87
    elisions   88
    spellings   89
    stage-directions   76n71
APOSTROPHES see also ELISIONS   10 33 52 87 89-90
APOSTROPHES, POSSESSIVE   46-7 90
ARDEN SHAKESPEARE   7 75
ASSEMBLED TEXTS see MASSED ENTRIES
AS YOU LIKE IT
    elisions   88
    spellings   89
Bald, R. C.   7
    Bibliographical Studies   23n32 133n142
    ed. Game at Chess   3n5 21n29 24
BARNAVELT, SIR JOHN VAN OLDEN   2 11 12-13 14 17n23 70 73 88 133
    book-keeper   6n11
    contractions   43
    elisions   45 46
    elisions, Jonsonian   44
    hyphenated-compounds   39 41
    parentheses   86
    parentheses, vocative   35
    punctuation   39 83 84
    speech-prefixes   27 30
    spellings   1n2 67
    stage-directions   3-6 22n30 26n37 123
Barroll, J. L.   34n41
Blayney, P. W. M.   99n101
Brown, J. R.   37n45 137n148 140n151
Bullen, A. H.   37n44
CAMBRIDGE SHAKESPEARE   118 119
CAPITALISATION   36 84
    of verse   36

CATCHWORDS 28
Chambers, sir E. K. 134n143 134n145
COLONS 38 85-6
COMEDY OF ERRORS
    elisions 88
   hyphenated-compounds 90
   spellings 89 95-6 166-7
   stage-directions 76 124
COMMAS 85-6
COMPOSITOR ANALYSIS 1n2
COMPOSITOR A
   2H6 76
   WT 123n135 130 130n139
COMPOSITOR A(F) see COMPOSITOR F
COMPOSITOR B
   Err. 76 95-6 124 166-7
   MM 98 124 127 170-1
   Shr. 96 97 167-9
   spellings 92-9
   stage-directions 81
   Tmp. 75 97 109 169-70
   TN 94-5 165-6
   Wiv. 79 81 98 121 170
   WT 96-7 123n135 130 171-2
COMPOSITOR C
   MM 77 123n135 126 127
   MV 76
   stage-directions 78
   TGV 77
   Tmp. 109 123n135
   Wiv. 121
COMPOSITOR D
   MM 123n134
COMPOSITOR F 77 79 89 130n139
   MM 123n135
   TGV 76 79
   Tmp. 123n135
COMPOSITORS 16-17 35 74
   hyphens 91
   mislining 109-10
   punctuation 84-5 86
   spellings 92-3 137
   stage-directions 78 123n135
COMPOUND VERB AUXILIARIES 46 51
CONTRACTIONS 43
CRANE, Ralph. (For transcripts and works associated with
    Crane, see under titles of works)

CRANE, Ralph cont.

    accuracy 55-61 133
    and his copy 5n9 13-14
    and Jonson 10 21
    and King's Men 1-2
    and prose 36-7
    as book-keeper 2-6
    calligraphy 13
    dedications 1n2 11-12
    dramatic transcripts 9-15 72-3
    handwriting 16-19 75-6
    influence in F1 7-8 69-103 138-9
    order of F transcripts 70-1 135-8
    punctuation 31-9 83-4 137
    Rejoinder 43
    scribal practices (see also under particular headings)
       16-68
    spellings 1n2 61-8
    spellings in F1 91-102 165-72
    stage-directions in transcripts 21-7
    Summary 61
    Works of Mercy 1-2
CYMBELINE 105n105 108
CYNTHIA'S REVELS 20
DEMETRIUS AND ENANTHE see also THE HUMOUROUS LIEUTENANT
    11 12 14 17n23 31 107
    elisions 45 46
    elisions, Jonsonian 44 51n53
    errors 55-6 59-60
    handwriting 17-18
    hyphenated-compounds 40 41
    parentheses 34
    parentheses, vocative 35
    punctuation 33 38
    speech-prefixes 28
    spellings 1n2 67
    stage-directions 22n30 23 26n37 124
    text 133 163-5
    watermarks 11n20
DIAERESES 10
DUCHESS OF MALFI, THE 10 78
    apostrophes 136
    elisions 136
    elisions, Jonsonian 136-7
    hyphens 136 136n147
    prose 37
    stage-directions 21 79 139-40

EDWARD III   111n118
ELISIONS see also APOSTROPHES 43-7 88-90
ELISIONS, JONSONIAN see also under titles 7 10 33
      44 137
ELISIONS AND METRE 51-3
EXCLAMATION MARKS 85
FIRST FOLIO see also CRANE - influence in F1;
      COMPOSITORS; and titles of individual texts
      6 6n11 7-8 34n41 61 66-7 68 70
   accidentals 75-81
   apostrophes 87-8
   elisions 88-90
   hyphenation 90-1
   punctuation 81-91
   spellings 91-102
   stage-directions 75-81
FLETCHER, John. For works, see under titles
FOLIO, FIRST see FIRST FOLIO
Frijlinck, Wilhelmina P.   1n2 3n6 17n23
GAME AT CHESS, A   3 11-12 137
      elisions 44 46 51
      elisions, Jonsonian 51
      hyphenated-compounds 41
      metre 47-53
      speech-prefixes 28-9
      stage-directions 5n9 25 26
GAME. Bridgewater Ms. 22 23 24
GAME. Folger Ms. 11 14 15 73 133
      act/scene headings 19
      apostrophes, possessive 47
      capitalisation 36
      catchwords 28
      elisions 46
      elisions, Jonsonian 44
      handwriting 31
      hyphenated-compounds 40 41 42
      metre 54
      parentheses, vocative 35
      punctuation 37-8
      sententia 10
      speech-prefixes 28-9
      spellings 1n2 67
      stage-directions 19 22 23-4 25 26 26n37 27
GAME. Lansdowne Ms. 11-12 14 131
      contractions 43
      elisions 45 46 51
      elisions, Jonsonian 44

INDEX 185

GAME. Lansdowne Ms. cont.

 errors 57-8
 handwriting 18
 hyphenated-compounds 40 41 42
 metre 54
 parentheses 34
 parentheses, vocative 35
 speech-prefixes 29
 spellings 1n2
 stage-directions 18 <u>21-3</u> 24 25 26 26n37 124
 text 160-1

GAME. Malone Ms. 12 14 72
 elisions 45 <u>51</u> 52
 elisions, Jonsonian 44
 errors 57-8
 hyphenated-compounds 40 41 42 136
 parentheses 34
 parentheses, vocative 35
 speech-prefixes 29
 spellings 1n2
 stage-directions 6-7 19-22 80 113 124 130 130n139 139
 text 160-1
 watermarks 11n20

GAME. Trinity Ms. 57 58
 act/scene headings 19
 capitalisation 36
 elisions 46
 elisions, Jonsonian 51
 stage-directions 22n30 <u>23-4</u> 25
 verse 37

GAME. 1625 Quartos 22 23 24 30
Gardner, dame Helen L. 7n12
Greg, sir W. W. 2-3 6-7 17n23 75
 ed. Book of sir T. More 29n38
 <u>Dramatic Documents.</u> 4 5n10
 <u>Editorial Problems</u> 107n109
 ed. Merry Wives 119n127
 <u>Shakespeare First Folio</u> 3n4 5n10 6n11 7n13 15n22 70n62 70n63 77n74 80n76 86n84 88 108n110 108n112 113n122 119n128 124n136 134n143 139
 Some notes ... Witch 40n48
 ed. The Witch 25n34 58
Harper, J. W. 38n46
<u>2 HENRY IV</u> 8n15 77
<u>HENRY V</u> 30

2 HENRY VI   76
HENRY VIII   105n105 108
Herford and Simpson. Ben Jonson   10n18 17n23 20n27
    44n50 44n51 55 56n58 128n138
Hinman, C. J. K.   1n2 14n21 70n64 70n66 77n73
Howard-Hill, T. H. Compositors of Sh. F comedies.
    122n132
    Knight, Crane & WT   6n11 130n140
    Ralph Crane's parentheses   34n40
    Spelling analysis & Crane   1n2 61n61
    Spelling & the bibliographer   1n2 92n92
HUMOUROUS LIEUTENANT, THE   59 133 163-5
HYPHENATED-COMPOUNDS see HYPHENATION and under titles
HYPHENATION   39-43 90-1
HYPHENS   33 39
HYPHENS, DOUBLE   10 15
ITALICISATION   17-18 30-1
JONSON, Benjamin see also ELISIONS, JONSONIAN. For
    works, see under titles. 44n50
    influence on Crane   10 21 139
Kable, W. S.   93n94 99n101
Kermode, J. F.   75n69 107n109 108n111 109n113 109n114
    110n115 111n116 111n118
KING JOHN   8n15
KING LEAR   133
KNIGHT, Edward   6n11
Kökeritz, H.   53n55 53n56
Leech, C.   113n121 114 114n124
Lever, J. W.   99 102 122 122n31 123n134 124 126 127
LINEATION   36-7
LOCALITY INDICATIONS   10
LONDON'S VISITATION   34
LOVE'S LABOUR'S LOST   128
McKerrow, R. B. Introduction to Bibliography   111n117
    136n147
    Prologomena   52n54
    A suggestion   29n39
Malone Society   9 17n23 39
MASQUE OF QUEENS, THE   10
MASSED ENTRIES   6 10 20-1 113n121
    in F1   79-80 139-40
MASSINGER, Philip. For works, see under titles
Maxwell, J. C.   111
MEASURE FOR MEASURE   1 69 78 80n76 108 122-8 137-8
    140
    apostrophes   128
    apostrophes, possessive   90

MEASURE FOR MEASURE cont.
    elisions, Jonsonian 89 128
    hyphens 127 128
    parentheses 86
    parentheses, vocative 87
    punctuation 83 84 85
    spellings 88 98 129 170-1
    stage-directions 77 79 122-3
    text 124-7 133
MERCHANT OF VENICE, THE 20 76
MERRY WIVES OF WINDSOR, THE 1 69 78 108 117-22 137-8
    apostrophes 117 118
    elisions, Jonsonian 117
    hyphens 117-8 129
    parentheses 87
    parentheses, vocative 87
    punctuation 84 85
    spellings 89 98 170
    stage-directions 21 77 79 81 107 118 130n139 139-40
    text 120-2 133 134 135 140
METRE see also under titles 43-4 47-54
MIDDLETON, Thomas. For works, see under titles 3 55
    elisions 44
    spellings 10 112n120
MUCH ADO ABOUT NOTHING 85
NAMES 18 31
NAMES OF THE ACTORS 10 77-8 80
Nosworthy, J. M. 8n15 55-6 59 60n60
OATHS see PROFANITY
Oliver, H. J. 8n15 119n129 122n130
OTHELLO 77
Pafford, J. H. P. 6n11 128 132n141
PARENTHESES 6 34-6 39 86-7
PARENTHESES, VOCATIVE 34-6 87
Partridge, A. C. 36n43 89n90
PERICLES 108
PLEASURE RECONCILED TO VIRTUE 9-11 14 17n23
    contractions 43
    elisions 45n52
    elisions, Jonsonian 44
    errors 56-7
    hyphenated-compounds 39 40 128 128n138
    metre 55
    parentheses 86
    punctuation 83 84
    spellings 1n2 67

POETASTER 20
Pollard, A. W. 108
POSSESSIVE APOSTROPHES see APOSTROPHES, POSSESSIVE
PROFANITY 133-5
PROSE 36-7
PUNCTUATION see also HYPHENATION and names of particular
      marks of punctuation, and under titles 31-9
      81-91
PUNCTUATION, DENSITY OF 38
QUOTATION MARKS 10
REJOINDER see CRANE
Rhodes, R. C. 20
ROMEO AND JULIET 79
RUNNING-TITLES 11
SEJANUS 20
SENTENTIA 10 137
'SEUERALLY' 22n30
Shaaber, M. A. 8n15
SHAKESPEARE, William. For works, see under titles
SIR THOMAS MORE 29n38 88n89 134 134n144
      elisions 89n90
      hyphens 91
      parentheses 87n85
      punctuation 85n83
      spellings 90
SONG IN SEVERAL PARTS, A 11
SPEECH-PREFIXES 27-31 57 58 59
SPEECH-RULES 27
SPELLING see CRANE. Spellings and under titles
STAGE-DIRECTIONS see MASSED ENTRIES, 'WITHIN' and under
      titles, e.g. FIRST FOLIO
SUMMARY see CRANE
TAMING OF THE SHREW, THE
      elisions 88
      spellings 96 97 167-9
TEMPEST, THE 1 15 69 71 105-12 137-8 140
      apostrophes 105-6
      as model for F 107-8
      elisions, Jonsonian 89 112
      hyphens 106-7 128n138
      metre 112
      mislining 109-10
      parentheses, vocative 87
      punctuation 84 85
      spellings 89 97 169-70
      stage-directions 75 77 78 79 108-9 113 139
      text 110-12 133

TIMON OF ATHENS 8n15 77
TWELFTH NIGHT 70
    elisions 88
    spellings 90 94-5 165-6
TWO GENTLEMEN OF VERONA, THE 1 69 71 92 99 108 112-17
    137-8
    apostrophes 114
    elisions 116-17
    hyphens 114 128n138
    parentheses, vocative 87
    punctuation 84 85
    spellings 89 90
    stage-directions 21 76 77 79 107 113 123 130n139
        139-40
    text 115-17 127 133 140
VOLPONE 20
Walker, Alice 93 135n146
WEBSTER, John. For works, see under titles
Wilson, F. P. 1-3 1n2 7 17n23 75
    Ralph Crane 1n1 4n8
    Shakespeare & new bibliography 3 6 7n12 7n14 21n28
    ed. Demetrius 25n35
Wilson, J. D. 6-7 20 21 75 79
    ed. Julius Caesar 104n104
    ed. Winter's Tale 26n36
WINTER'S TALE, THE 1 14 36 69 70 71 77 77n74 108
    128-37 137-8 139
    apostrophes 129
    elisions, Jonsonian 129
    hyphens 117 129
    parentheses 86
    parentheses, vocative 87
    punctuation 83 84 85
    spellings 89 96-7 171-2
    stage-directions 21 79 80 129-31 140
    text 131-5 140
WITCH, THE 11 14 17n23 78 107 133
    act/scene headings 19
    elisions 46
    elisions, Jonsonian 44
    errors 56 58-9 59n59
    handwriting 18
    hyphenated-compounds 40 41 42
    parentheses, vocative 35
    prose 36
    punctuation 33
    speech-prefixes 28

WITCH, THE cont.

    spellings 1n2 67
    stage-directions 24n33 26n37 58-9
    text 161-3
    watermarks 11
'WITHIN' STAGE-DIRECTIONS 123-4
WORKS OF MERCY see CRANE